P9-DDY-789

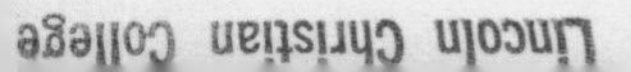
Lincoln Christian College

Exploring the Small Community

Otto G. Hoiberg

UNIVERSITY OF NEBRASKA PRESS

Publishers on the Plains
UNP

Library of Congress Catalogue Card Number 55-8933
Manufactured in the United States of America

TO

DAGMAR

FOREWORD

The author of *Exploring the Small Community* is ideally fitted by family background, education, and experience to develop the theme on which this book is based. He has lived in several small Midwest communities and is the son of a Danish Lutheran minister who ardently believed in the soundness of his native country's folk high schools. The father, in fact, successfully operated two such schools in America and while he lived made them thriving and vital educational institutions.

Dr. Hoiberg earned his doctorate in sociology at the University of Nebraska, working with men who have a realistic and constructive attitude toward rural life. Then he taught for several years in college and university. In 1945 he went to Germany, where for three years he helped that country rebuild its religious institutions in the period of near-chaos immediately following World War II. Coming back to his alma mater in 1948, he established a bureau of community service and without fanfare but with boundless energy and quiet enthusiasm set out to work with the towns and villages of his state. During the years that have passed since 1948 Dr. Hoiberg has been invited to scores of Nebraska communities, usually first for a preliminary conference to discuss problems and possibilities, and then to advise periodically in the ways and means of achieving the objectives decided upon.

The author is not one who believes that democracy in the United States is wholly dependent upon what the small community does. He does believe, however, that democracy will be greatly strengthened or weakened as small communities grow strong or become weak. He has no magic formula for improving small community life. Dr. Hoiberg holds, and this book bears out this point of view, that success in the betterment of our small communities rests upon a clear understanding of the procedures to be followed, the formulation of worthwhile and attainable goals, and the patience and understanding needed to reach those goals one step at a time. He recognizes that citizens of small communities are typically intelligent and well-educated people of good will, and that the problems of small community life need only the thoughtful approach that any other problem requires. Point by point and subject by subject this theme is developed on the pages that follow.

One need not conjecture whether the philosophy of Dr. Hoiberg is sound. The results already obtained in his work with small communities are ample evidence of that soundness.

This book should have a large audience. It was not written in the technical language which would limit its use to the professional sociologist. It is for him, of course, but even more for the citizens in small communities, of which there are tens of thousands who want very much to make their community the better and more beautiful place they know it can be. This book points the way.

KNUTE O. BROADY

Lincoln, Nebraska
May, 1955.

PREFACE

This book has been written primarily for people of rural communities throughout the nation who are working at the great task of community improvement. Its purpose is to help them visualize more clearly some of the paths that are open to them in their quest for richer group living. It may also be of interest as supplementary reading matter for students of rural sociology and as a source of information for Extension workers and others who are professionally concerned with the small community.

Essentially the volume is an outgrowth of seven years of field work done by the author under the community service program of the University of Nebraska Extension Division. No effort at exhaustive treatment of the various subject areas has been made. In general, the discussion has been geared to existing major needs of small communities, as sensed by the author in his contacts with them. Many of the illustrations have been drawn from personal experience in Nebraska communities in order to assure maximum authenticity. It is felt that rural communities throughout many parts of the United States have common elements sufficiently numerous to make such illustrations relevant on a broader basis.

Part I deals with some of the processes which appear significant in relation to community improvement programs. Part II gives attention to specific problem areas, with particular reference to solutions which have been tried.

Sincere gratitude is expressed to the following individuals, who read the manuscript and offered helpful criticism: Dr. Harold F. Kaufman, Mississippi State College; Mr. A. H. Anderson, Royal Commission on Agriculture and Rural Life, Saskatchewan; Dr. Paul Meadows, University of Nebraska; and Dr. K. O. Broady, University of Nebraska. The last deserves special thanks for constant encouragement.

Appreciation is expressed also to the various publishers for permission to use quotations which seemed essential to the purpose of this book. Finally, the author is indebted to Mrs. Frances E. McCall for typing the manuscript and to his wife and four sons for accepting rain checks in lieu of many traditional family activities during the past year.

O. G. H.

Lincoln, Nebraska
May, 1955

CONTENTS

(continued)

(contents continued)

PART TWO

Problem Areas

PART ONE

ESSENTIALS OF COMMUNITY IMPROVEMENT

1

UNDERSTANDING THE SMALL COMMUNITY

Ideas are the mightiest influence on earth.—W. H. CHANNING

DURING RECENT YEARS there has been a growing interest throughout the United States in *the community* and its problems.

Social scientists have expanded their research activities in this subject area, and much is being done through University Extension and other educational channels to bring the data thus acquired to the community action groups which can use them.

Diverse organizations of broad scope are making efforts to stimulate and facilitate community improvement activities at the grass roots through contests, literature, radio, TV, and in some instances through actual community consultation work.

Observe, for example, the annual community development prizes awarded by the National Grange, the work of the General Federation of Women's Clubs in sponsoring community improvement contests, the community development program of the Georgia Power Company, and the television and radio series of the Ford Foundation entitled, respectively, "The Whole Town's Talking" and "The People Act."

Communities themselves are displaying an increasing interest in the concept of *planning* for more abundant and effective social living, in preference to the "Topsy-like" approach which has characterized so much of our community development in the past.

One might venture a guess as to why this growth of interest has occurred. Is it a fad which will eventually run its course and then sink into oblivion, or are we actually witnessing a long-term social movement with a future? There is reason to believe that the latter may be the case, because the values concerned are so intimately related to the troubled world situation which confronts us.

There has been a tendency in the past to assume that the continued existence and gradual spread of the democratic way of life could be taken for granted. People throughout the world would move in a very natural way toward this desirable type of society, given time and opportunity to learn of its qualities. This, however, has proved to be an oversimplification. Whatever the reasons may be, democracy today finds itself locked in mortal combat with a powerful opposing ideology, the totalitarian, and the ultimate victory of democracy in the minds of men is by no means a foregone conclusion.

A growing recognition of this fact has led to much serious thought and action in the United States. Our approach to the problem has been twofold. First, we have moved to strengthen ourselves in a physical sense. Our expenditures for military purposes have reached almost astronomical proportions and we have acquired a fighting machine on land, sea and in the air that is second to none. We realize, however, that military strength is not enough. It can become a factor in the ideological struggle only in the sense that it serves to keep the mailed fist of totalitarianism at bay, giving the constructive democratic forces an opportunity to work.

Our second approach has been in the field of human relationships, where the ultimate strength of any nation lies. We have recognized anew the necessity for making better citizens and building stronger communities, and it is probably here that one finds the real explanation of our increased interest and activity along community development lines.

Of special concern in this book are the small community in

agricultural regions and its efforts to provide a wholesome and satisfying mode of living in a complex and rapidly changing world. Two generations ago Theodore Roosevelt's Commission on Country Life stressed the vital importance of endeavoring to overcome the deficiencies of rural living, and much progress has certainly been made since that day. A great deal remains to be done, however, before rural America can be considered as utilizing fully the many resources for good living which are at its disposal.

One of the prime essentials for continued improvement is a realistic interpretation of the contemporary small community by the rural people themselves. In many quarters a pessimism prevails which often leads to inaction and aimless drifting. In one such locality, a long-time resident said in a disheartened tone: "Thirty years ago we had a thriving little community here. Business was good, there was lots of stuff going on, and it was really an interesting place to live . . . But just look at us today! I tell you, in another thirty years there won't be *anything* left around here."

It is surely not without reason that people living in small communities sometimes wonder what will eventually become of their way of life. Decade after decade the U. S. Census has shown a relentless trend toward urbanization. At the beginning of the twentieth century 60 per cent of the total U. S. population was classified as rural, a figure which by 1950 had fallen to 36 per cent. The farm element of the rural population fell from 34 per cent of the nation's population in 1910 to 15 per cent in 1950, and in addition revealed a decline in absolute numbers. Although the total population of the United States increased by nearly 59 million between 1910 and 1950, there were actually four million fewer people living on farms at the end of this period than at its beginning.

Nearly four of every ten non-suburban villages of 250 to 999 population experienced population decreases for the decade 1940-1950. During the same period, incorporated hamlets (below 250 population) continued their downward trend, 64 per cent of them sustaining losses.[1]

Of obvious concern to many is also the fact that open country churches with their rich, informal fellowship seem to be losing their foothold. Further, the country schoolhouse, which has often been a significant social center, as well as a place for educating youngsters, is yielding to a movement for consolidation which holds great promise for the improvement of rural educational opportunities, to be sure, but which tends to hasten the disintegration of the traditional open-country neighborhood.

It is important, however, for rural Americans to view *in full context* the seemingly disturbing aspects of trends such as these. The over-all situation of the rural community is by no means as ominous as it may sometimes appear. Granted that the communities centered about very small trade centers are having a relatively difficult time in holding their own, population-wise the current trend of medium and larger villages is anything but discouraging. More than 47 per cent of all non-suburban villages with populations ranging from 1,000 to 2,500 gained 10 per cent or more in population from 1940 to 1950, and, in fact, "enjoyed a greater amount of growth . . . than in any previous decade since 1910, when separate tabulations were first made."[2]

Even where population loss occurs, it does not necessarily mean that a community is waning. Fortunately there is no inherent relation between the quality of community living and size of population. Sound physical growth is a fine thing for a community, but it is erroneous to assume that numerical increase inevitably implies the development of richer human relationships. People speak so glibly of a "declining" community where succeeding censuses have recorded drops in

1. Edmund de S. Brunner, "The Small Village, 1940-1950," *Rural Sociology,* June, 1952, pp. 127-31.
2. John H. Kolb and Edmund de S. Brunner, *A Study of Rural Society* (New York: Houghton Mifflin Co., 1952), p. 190.

population. "There must be something wrong with a place that is losing population!" Perhaps there is, but on the other hand it is possible that the numerically smaller community in question may actually be a better place in which to live than it would have been if the population decline had not occurred. In many instances, the decrease is simply a normal adjustment to the mechanization of agriculture with its consequent displacement of farm population.

During the nineteenth century when the little country of Denmark was passing through a most difficult phase of her history, a slogan was born which urged the Danes to convert "outward loss to inner gain." Many small communities in the United States would do well to keep this helpful maxim in mind. Enrichment of community living can occur even where population shows a downward trend. It must also be remembered that changes in rural institutions such as church, school, and place of business, however disconcerting they may be, often create new opportunities for better living when approached in a positive frame of mind.

Some time ago a German sociologist wrote a book[3] in which he distinguished between two kinds of social relationships. The one kind, *family-like* in nature, is characterized by informality, close personal feelings, and a broad mutual concern among the various members of a group. Its truest expression is found in the relation of a mother to her child, but it prevails also in considerable measure in other groups, such as the clique and the small community.

The second kind of relationship has been described as *contractual*,[4] which means that the members of a group have joined ranks to attain certain goals and that the relationships estab-

3. Ferdinand Toennies, *Fundamental Concepts of Sociology* (Gemeinschaft und Gesellschaft), translated by C. P. Loomis (New York: American Book Co., 1940).
4. C. P. Loomis and J. A. Beegle, *Rural Social Systems* (New York: Prentice-Hall, Inc., 1950), pp. 782-84.

lished are regarded as means to ends rather than as ends in themselves. Examples of this relationship are found in any professional organization and in the impersonal social phenomenon known as the city.

The emphasis which sociologists have placed upon these two concepts in recent years is probably not entirely academic. It reflects a concern over the current tendency of the contractual type of social relationship to displace the family-like variety, which for so long has been recognized as a fountainhead of values and personal qualities that are fundamental to our democratic society. It is a basic assumption of the present work that the small community with its informal, personal atmosphere has an important and continuing role to play in American life. An effort will be made to help the small community visualize more clearly the nature and social significance of this role and to offer information and suggestions which may be of assistance to it in its efforts to make life more gratifying and productive.

It is unwise to look with nostalgic eyes upon the rural community of yesteryear. In many respects the "good old days" have acquired a halo status that is out of harmony with the facts and, in any event, the future lies ahead. It is equally unwise to view with alarm the trend toward urbanization. What is actually occurring is a synthesis, or blending, of the various phases of urban and rural living, and it is entirely possible for the small community to acquire many desirable cultural characteristics in common with urban centers and still retain its distinctive family-like nature.

When a small community attempts to explore the many fascinating possibilities for strengthening its way of life, it is helpful to have a clear understanding of its own nature as a social entity. The difficulty of defining the concept *community* is reflected not only in the wide variety of versions developed by sociologists but also in the puzzling practical situations which frequently confront people who are outside the academic world.

In a rural trade center located about fifteen miles from a city of 100,000 population, for example, the villagers and farmers were working on the constitution for a new Community Club which was in process of formation. All were agreed that membership should be limited to people who belonged to their community, but they were at a loss as to how to delineate their community geographically. A number of folks who lived in the little town looked upon it mostly as a bedroom, since their work and most of their interests were centered in the nearby city; they were hardly thought of as members of the community. On the other hand, there were several people residing and working in the city who had grown up in the small community and who displayed their continued loyalty to it by commuting regularly from the city for church services, informal visiting, and other kinds of social activities. It was finally agreed that anyone who was interested in joining the new club would be considered eligible, the assumption being that the very desire to join would be sufficient evidence of membership in the community.

No effort will be made here to define the term "small community." It is essential, however, to indicate how the concept will be employed in the following pages. As already stated, we are concerned primarily with the small community in agricultural regions of the United States, the chief characteristics of which may be described briefly as follows:

It is a natural area. The small community ordinarily does not conform to legally defined boundaries of any kind. It comprises an incorporated or unincorporated trade center with a surrounding agricultural area which may take almost any shape, depending upon factors such as the location of adjoining trade centers, rivers, and highways. Regardless of size and shape, it consists of townspeople and farm people, living together in what might well be termed a *social watershed*. Primarily, we have in mind those communities which are formed around trade centers of 2,500 population or less, although much of what will be said in succeeding chapters may be relevant to somewhat larger communities as well.

It provides a core of services. A second characteristic of the small community is that it provides at least a minimum core of services for its people. No rigid list can be established as necessary for a social grouping to qualify as a community, but certainly some services of an economic, educational, religious, and recreational nature will ordinarily be included. In places which are incorporated, the governmental service is also prominent.

Many rural people still live in open-country neighborhoods which center about a church, a schoolhouse, or a country store, and while these are often referred to as communities by the people who live there, the term "open-country neighborhood" is undoubtedly more appropriate because the number of services provided is relatively limited.

It is characterized by a sense of belonging. People who live in a community have a feeling of belonging together. There is a generalized emotional involvement which serves to reinforce, as it were, the bonds which are established among community members through their business, church, school, and other activities. This is true in a very special sense of the small community with its close personal relationships. In an urban setting the individual citizen also has a feeling of "belonging," but it is a relatively impersonal reaction which is hardly reflected in his attitude toward the fellow citizen whom he meets on the street.

Baker Brownell states that when a group of people living in a given locality becomes so large that the individuals no longer know each other, there can be no talk of community.[5] Community is essentially a personal relationship among people who

5. Baker Brownell, *The Human Community* (New York: Harper & Brothers, 1950), p. 207.

live together, and where for any reason the relationship becomes impersonal, community ceases to exist. There are other authors who regard the term as applicable also to larger social groupings, but the small community which concerns us here falls well within the scope of Brownell's concept.

A serious obstacle to self-improvement of the small community has been the widespread belief that "we know our community." In reality, most rural people do not know their own communities. This has been revealed time and again where community self-study projects have been conducted, as one was recently in Eldorado, Illinois. Here an intensive and comprehensive research program was carried on by local citizens with the cooperation of the Department of Community Development of Southern Illinois University. Through this process they learned a great deal about themselves that they had never known before, and with a clearer perspective of themselves as a community, they were then in position to attack intelligently and with enthusiasm the job of making Eldorado a better place in which to live.

Every sound community improvement program rests upon an understanding of the physical and human resources which are available to the community and of the forces that operate within it.

2

COMMUNITY PLANNING: THE CONCEPT

Light tomorrow with today!—E. B. BROWNING

REDUCED TO SIMPLEST TERMS, community planning is the systematic application of forethought to the problems of community development. That such forethought should be applied may seem axiomatic to the reader, and yet the small communities are legion in which serious consideration is given to civic problems only as they arise and become acute. Despite lip service to the contrary, they make no consistent effort to anticipate their problems and to plan for the future. Partly responsible for this situation are three common misconceptions regarding community planning.

First, there is the notion that planning is an urban phenomenon which does not make sense in the rural community. In days of yore, many cities were built according to plans which provided for defense against enemies or for civic beauty. In the contemporary urban world, we find more and more comprehensive city plans which give the technical guidance necessary for orderly growth. From time immemorial, however, the rural community has plodded along informally, and even today it is widely regarded as a social unit which will take care of itself without much ado.

Actually, the concept of planning has as much to offer in the rural setting as in the urban. The practice of looking ahead and working toward carefully established community goals is desirable in both instances, and while the strategy must be adapted to the peculiar needs of each situation, the underlying principles are identical.

A second misconception holds that community planning is an academic sort of thing which is of interest only to certain long-haired professors who live in ivory towers. It is true that writings exist on this subject which employ terminology that is bewildering to the uninitiated, but this should not be cause for concern. Every practical social program has its theoretical background, and theoretical writings are quite naturally phrased in language that is intelligible only to people who are professionally trained in the discipline concerned.

Community planning is a very down-to-earth approach to the improvement of community living. Every sound business firm plans in a practical way for the future. Every well-integrated family works systematically toward clearly defined goals which it has set for itself. Why should a community not do the same? There is nothing visionary at all about this approach. It is just good common sense applied to the problems of everyday group living.

A third erroneous idea is that community planning is expensive. Wherever the planning concept enters the picture, it is feared the community is in for a wild spending spree which may bring grand improvements, to be sure, but only at the expense of solvency. A moment's reflection will show the fallacy of this line of thought. Spending money without regard to financial resources is anything *but* planning, and any community which proceeds in this manner betrays a total ignorance of the planning concept. A community which plans will study carefully its current and estimated future financial resources and provide for the economical use of such resources in the attainment of desirable goals over a period of time. Improvements will be scheduled in an orderly manner, high-priority items coming first, and the rate of progress will at all times be realistically geared to the availability of funds and to the over-all financial situation of the community.

Planning is a long-term proposition. Money is spent today for conducting basic studies and developing action plans which will save the community money tomorrow. As indicated in Chapter 1, there is every reason to believe that the small community is here to stay, and if this is so, it would seem advisable to give due consideration to the generations to come rather than devote all attention to the contemporary scene. An intelligent person tries to refrain from spending his entire income on goods for immediate consumption; he invests a reasonable proportion with an eye to future satisfactions. By the same token, the progressive community makes a policy of investing a part of its current revenue in activities which are designed to enrich community living in years that lie ahead. Community planning is just such an investment.

It is often hazardous to divide a continuous process into component parts. In order to identify the various phases of the community planning process, however, let us attempt this, recognizing that the three phases to be discussed are closely interrelated and that there are no clearly defined lines of demarcation between them. The first phase of any planning program has to do with fact-finding; the second, with the development of a "paper plan"; and the third, with the problem of implementation.[1] This is true whether one is thinking of a comprehensive plan whose scope includes all areas of community living, or merely of a plan developed to improve, let us say, the school system, the recreational program, or the physical appearance of a town. Let us take a brief look at each of these in turn.

1. The author recognizes that implementation, strictly speaking, is not a part of the planning process. In view of the close integration which exists between these two aspects of the total action process in any practical situation, however, the term community planning has been interpreted broadly here to encompass both.

Fact Finding. Enthusiasm for a community improvement program is a fine thing, but if it is not to misfire, it must be undergirded with a store of factual information pertinent to the topic at hand. Many well-meaning groups have learned the hard way that it is difficult indeed to build a stable and enduring program without first acquiring certain basic data to guide them in their endeavors.

Hospitals have sometimes been built in a period of emotional upsurge, for example, only to close their doors again because there were not enough patients to keep such an institution alive. Many ill-fated community councils have been organized by people who developed an emotional attachment to the idea without taking the trouble to find out whether the various groups involved really needed and wanted any such arrangement at all. Or, witness a rapidly deteriorating community hall which was erected with no thought whatever as to what it would cost to maintain the completed building or how the money for this purpose was to be raised. It is well to remember the old adage: Look before you leap! And it might be added that the look should be somewhat more than casual. We know, of course, that obstructionists sometimes utilize a "need for more facts" purely as a stalling device, but even more dangerous to community welfare is the person who pushes for action before the group has any real understanding of the fundamental factors concerned.

All good community planning begins with fact-finding of one type or another. The first step taken by a newly organized planning commission in a small town is often to identify the problems which the people consider most urgent. Figures 1 and 2 show simple questionnaires, either of which can be circulated for this purpose. With top-priority items thus brought to light, the fact-finding activities can then be focussed upon the specific problems, such as new street lights, a sewer system, or parking meters, which are considered most important. If an

FIGURE 1

Community Planning Commission
Smalltown, U.S.A.

Gentlemen:

In my opinion, the most urgent needs of our community are the following:

____

____

____

____

____
Sign only if you wish

over-all community plan is to be developed, the studies will naturally deal with all major areas of community living.

The small community is often in need of technical assistance in relation to its fact-finding activities. Where this is true, a

FIGURE 2

HOW DO WE RATE IN SMALLTOWN, U.S.A.?

Instructions: Place a check mark in the blank space opposite each item which most nearly represents your opinion. If you wish to comment, please use space provided below:

Item	Excellent	Adequate	Inadequate	Very Inadequate
1. Business: goods and services provided by our business firms				
2. Cultural opportunities: music, art, drama, etc.				

Item	Excellent	Adequate	Inadequate	Very Inadequate
3. Education: our school buildings and program				
4. Facilities for medical and dental care				
5. Physical appearance: attractiveness and neatness of our town				
6. Protection against hazards: traffic, fire, health, etc.				
7. Recreation: facilities and program for old and young				
8. Religion: opportunities for religious worship and fellowship				
9. Streets and parking facilities				
10. Coordination of community Activities				
11. Community spirit				
12. Other items (specify):				

Comments, if any:

____
Sign only if you wish

Please return to: _______________

logical first approach is to the state university or to some other public agency. If someone must be employed to do the research, there will be commercial firms available.

Project or Program Planning. Every study, no matter how carefully executed, has capacity to gather dust on a shelf. That is precisely what happens in far too many instances. Important as the fact-finding phase of the community planning process is, its principal function is to provide the foundation for an ensuing action program. Where the latter fails to materialize, the research cannot be said to have served the purpose for which it was intended.

This is in no sense a reflection on the concept of "pure research," where investigations are conducted with no eye whatever to the practical use of data gathered. An elderly biology professor who was deeply absorbed in the study of a microscopic animal was once asked why on earth he was spending his time on *that*. "Don't ask me why!" he replied. "My only reason for doing it is that I want to know more about this little creature!" In a similar manner, there are scholars the country over who are devoting time and effort to scientific research on community life simply because they desire to gain a deeper understanding of what makes a community tick. Whether a researcher is concentrating his attention upon a minute biological organism or upon a pattern of human relationships, his findings accrue from a sheer love of learning, not from an urge to contribute toward the solution of any given problem. This type of research must be encouraged because it contributes to the store of information about man and his world, and, as such, is intimately related to the long-term progress of human society.

The type of research which we have in mind in the present connection, however, is geared directly to a specific problem of community improvement, and here obviously it is unfortunate when the findings are not brought to bear upon the issue at hand. A plan of action must be devised which is based upon careful analysis of the factual information gathered, that is, upon a diagnosis of the situation concerned.

In developing the plan of action, as in gathering the facts, undue haste should be avoided. Many errors in planning are traceable to overenthusiasm for immediate action. The goal looms large ahead, and there is impatience with the "crepe hanger" who feels that more groundwork is needed prior to concrete action. A case in point is a community (village population, about 200) which had reached the conclusion that a community council should be organized. Everything seemed favorable for launching this enterprise, with one exception: the highly influential woman's club was not a participant in the project. However, rather than take a little more time to educate the leader of the club regarding the community council proposal and to allay certain misgivings which she was known to possess, the new organization was launched with the woman's club on the sidelines and negatively inclined toward the whole development. Within a year, the community council had faded from the scene, largely because of passive resistance from the woman's club. Perhaps this community council should never have been started. On the other hand, it might well have become an effective group if the enthusiasts had made haste a little more slowly.

A second important thing to remember is that all pertinent facts must be brought into the open and viewed objectively while the plan of action is being laid. In a town of 1,600 population, plans for the construction of a community hall were progressing rapidly, spearheaded by a group of volunteers. Certainly there was a real need for a community hall, but the town also happened to be in need of a school auditorium because a portion of the existing building had recently been condemned. Could the people of this locality finance both a community hall and a school auditorium? If not, would it be best to build a community hall which could also be used for school purposes, or a school auditorium which would be available for community activities? The importance of these questions was obvious, but the members of the community hall committee had their hearts very much set on their project and apparently feared that asking too many questions might delay action and perhaps even lead to the shelving of their plans in favor of some alternative scheme. Fortunately, however, they changed their slant on the situation, and before a final decision was made, the whole issue had been openly and thoroughly discussed jointly by the community hall committee, the city council, and the school board, all of whom were deeply concerned, regardless of what course of action might eventually be taken.

An interesting example of how this second phase of the planning process works was found in a western Nebraska town, Broken Bow, where the Planning Commission of nine members concentrated on the task of developing plans for a new park-playground area. All facts needed had been gathered. Before them lay a contour map of the cornfield which had been selected as the site for the new park area. They had a list of the different facilities which were desired in the park by the people of the community. The problem at hand was to develop a satisfactory "blueprint" which could be followed as a guide in construction. This was done by cutting pieces of blue construction paper, drawn to scale, to represent the tennis courts and other activities for which provision was to be made. These were placed on the contour map, and heavy yarn was stretched around pins to represent roads. After several hours of discussion and exploratory shifting of the various items into all sorts of arrangements, agreement was reached on a pattern which seemed to satisfy the needs. Subsequently the proposed layout was checked by a professionally trained person and revised in the light of his suggestions. Finally, the plan was submitted by the Planning Commission to the Park Board with the recommendation that it be adopted as the long-term plan for the future development of their community park.

Where a comprehensive community plan is concerned, the blueprint will deal with numerous phases of community living rather than with a single one. In any case, however, this second part of the planning process results in the formulation of a plan of action.

Implementation. Perhaps the most difficult task of all is to get the plan "off paper." One reason for this is that while the fact-finding and project-planning functions can often be done effectively by small groups of devoted citizens, the problem of implementation is community-wide in nature.

A banker from a midwestern city recently said to the author: "Yes, we have a nice, comprehensive plan all worked out for the development of our city during the next twenty-five years, but the trouble is that we aren't using it!" One may surmise that vested interests are partly responsible for a situation like this, but it is also probable that a lack of public understanding and support of the plan is an underlying factor. Even in an urban area with all its governmental machinery and technical specialists, a city plan is doomed if the citizens as a whole do not become interested and actively involved.

But broad involvement is particularly urgent in the small community, because so much of the community improvement effort there is of a voluntary nature. Countless projects in rural areas are not dependent in any way upon tax funds and public officials, and even where they are, voluntary contributions often play a supporting role. A town of 1,353 population (Sutton, Nebraska) recently voted bonds for the construction of a swimming pool, and within one month after the bond election the farmers of the trade area had sponsored a money-raising event and were able to hand the mayor a check for $1,500 to help pay for the project.

In most progressive rural communities, there is a strong feeling of individual responsibility for the general welfare and a willingness of the average citizen to assume his share of the work load. Here lies the secret of successful implementation of the rural community plan. Without this spirit of active participation, the small community stagnates because the leaders can't do it all, and ordinarily there are insufficient funds to hire outsiders for the work to be done.

There is an old legend which relates that a king was to visit his subjects in an area of rich vineyards. The local committee in charge of the celebration decided that the most appropriate way of paying homage to their king would be to present him with a vat of their finest wines. Each citizen was therefore asked to contribute a small quantity as his share of the superb gift. On the great day the king ceremoniously sipped the wine which had been given to him, and his joy turned to wrath! It seems that each person in the locality had poured a highly diluted contribution into the vat, assuming that this would not be noticed when all his neighbors gave of their best. The trouble was that his neighbors were all like him. . . . This type of thing is unfortunate in a city. In a rural community it is fatal.

Another important point to remember in implementing a community plan is that a timetable is ordinarily required. Some projects are of short duration and can be completed as a unit. Many others must unfold over a period of time, and here it becomes important to establish priorities in order that first things may come first. It is common knowledge that when a group tries to do too many things at once, it is apt to bog down and get nothing done at all.

Further, there is the matter of publicity. The writer knows of a hospital project which failed to materialize largely because the planning committee kept everything a deep, dark secret until popular suspicion and rumor had reached the point where general sentiment had crystallized against the proposal. They had intended to "spring" the full-blown project on the public, but learned to their dismay that the public should have been taken into their confidence from the very beginning. Americans are basically a reasonable lot and can be expected to act intelligently when they have the facts before them. This is a premise upon which our democratic form of government rests.

3

COMMUNITY PLANNING: THE PRACTICE

He would fain be at the top of the house before the stairs are built.—JONATHAN SWIFT

ONE OF THE INTERESTING THINGS about the community planning concept is that it lends itself to implementation through a variety of structures. There is no single organizational framework that is essential to its success. In fact, there is no particular type of planning mechanism which is suitable for all rural communities, because communities differ so widely. Scores of illustrations could be given, for example, of localities where community councils function superbly as planning agencies, but there are others in which they do not seem to be effective.

It is well to remember that it is the planning *process* which is important; the structure is only a means to an end. The goals and functions of community planning, as sketched in the previous chapter, are essentially the same everywhere, but each community must determine the form of organization which is best adapted to their implementation.

No effort will be made here to present an exhaustive list of the planning arrangements which are found in rural communities throughout the nation. Instead, we shall try to describe only a few of the more common approaches.

Probably the most widespread practice is to have no over-all body at all with responsibility for community planning. In this case, the local governmental authorities and the various voluntary organizations with an interest in civic improvement operate independently of each other on projects in which they have a special interest. The town board may thus develop a long-term plan for paving streets; the Chamber of Commerce may work on a program for expanding the trade area; and the Garden Club may give its attention over a period of years to a plan for beautification of the village.

These organizations may or may not follow sound planning procedures in relation to their respective projects, but, in any event, they can hardly be called planning agencies. The local governmental authorities in a small town, for example, are ordinarily so absorbed with the routine "musts" of their work that the research and deliberation essential to the planning task are hardly possible. Projects are apt to be launched piecemeal when pressure is greatest and with insufficient attention to their relation to other current or future needs.

One of the principal difficulties with this type of arrangement is the customary lack of coordination. One body may be at work on plans for a new sewerage system while others are busy promoting the construction of a swimming pool and a new community hall. Since money for public improvements rarely flows freely in the small community, complications often arise where such competing projects are under way. It makes little difference whether the proposed improvements involve tax funds, voluntary contributions, or both, because the money comes out of the same pockets in the final analysis. Each proposed community betterment project should be considered in the light of all others, and it is here that the idea of an over-all community planning agency becomes important.

The community council is perhaps the best known example of a body which provides such over-all coordination in rural areas. It has additional functions, to be sure, but these will be treated in Chapter 4. The structure of a community council is well adapted to the planning function. Its membership ordinarily includes a representative or two from each organized group in town and country which is actively interested in problems of community improvement. This gives the council a cross-sectional quality which is highly valuable where a well-rounded approach is desired. Furthermore, the council is not primarily an action group; this means that its major efforts can be devoted to fact finding and thorough discussion, both of which are frequently slighted by bodies which also have responsibility for action programs.

Deshler, Nebraska (population 1,063), provides an interesting example of how a community council can serve as a planning agency. For many years their public library had been housed in a room made available by the local parochial school, but this was too good to last. Time came when it was needed for other purposes, and abruptly a problem of community-wide proportions confronted them. There appeared to be no solution, except to pack their treasured volumes in boxes for storage in someone's basement—and this was no solution at all in the minds of the Deshler people.

The local Library Board turned logically to the Community Council, of which it was a member. In the discussions which followed, two things became clear. First, there was general agreement that the library was a valuable community asset which under no circumstances should be taken out of circulation; and second, it was felt that a library building project was possible but that it would require the full support of all interested groups in order to be successful.

The Deshler Community Council gave the library problem top-priority and then went to work on the arduous task of gathering data. What type of building would serve their library needs most effectively? Should facilities for Boy Scouts or other activities be included? What would an adequate building cost? What effect would a bond issue of "X" dollars have on the taxes paid in town? How had other communities proceeded under similar circumstances?

With the help of various outside agencies the answers to such questions were obtained, and when the building project proved to be feasible in the light of the facts, the Community Council systematically set out to place all pertinent information before the public as a guide to intelligent voting in the forthcoming bond election. All angles were clarified at meetings of the Community Council, and each representative relayed the information personally back to his own organization, where further discussions took place.

Gradually the plans for the new library took shape—a *community* project in every sense of the word. The vote was overwhelmingly favorable, and today an attractive new building serves as a focal point for cultural activities in the Deshler area.

The role of the community council as a planning agency in this instance comprised three major functions: (1) it gathered and analyzed factual data pertinent to the project; (2) it helped to develop a blueprint and a pattern of action; and (3) it played an influential part in converting the dream into reality by involving the entire community in the project.

A second arrangement for over-all planning provides for a regular "planning commission" as an integral part of the local government. This setup is seldom found in the smaller rural communities, but is not uncommon in towns of the 2,000-2,500 category. The movement received a substantial impetus in 1928, when a Standard City Planning Enabling Act was drawn up by the United States Department of Commerce. That model document has become the basis for enabling acts passed in a large number of states which, in turn, have made possible the formation of planning commissions in municipalities.

A typical state enabling act based on the Standard Act would enable any municipality to create a planning commission with authority to develop and adopt a city plan for the city and its surrounding area. After adoption of the city plan, all improvements of the types covered therein would have to be submitted in advance to the planning commission by the particular governmental units (school board, etc.) sponsoring the proposals. In case the planning commission found any proposal to be out of harmony with the city plan and therefore refused to approve it, the sponsoring agency would be able to override the disapproval by a two-thirds vote. Under the provisions of the Standard Act, the planning commission would have clear-cut responsibility in relation to zoning.

The specific structure and functions of a planning commission in any given municipality will of course be spelled out in a city ordinance drafted in accordance with the enabling act of that particular state. Whatever the legally defined duties of a planning commission in a small city may be, it will do well to keep the following guideposts in mind:

—It should have a clear understanding of its functions and procedures.

—Its basic concern should be with the welfare of the community as a whole. The commission must not, wittingly or unwittingly, become a tool of any special-interest group.

—Care must be taken to maintain effective liaison with the mayor and city council. A planning commission which cuts itself adrift from these local governmental authorities and becomes a pressure group (as sometimes happens) cannot serve the purpose for which it was intended.

—The activities of the planning commission should originate not only through requests and suggestions received from local governmental units and from other local agencies interested in problems of community improvement, but also through the initiative and insight of the planning commission itself.

—The planning commission should be a strong advocate of community planning and should exert a continuous educational influence toward this end.

As pointed out above, the community planning concept makes sense in the small community as well as in urban areas. The question may now be asked: Is planning essential in *all* rural communities, or do we find only certain types in which this kind of thing is desirable? In seeking an answer, let us glance consecutively at the growing, the declining, and the stationary community and observe how the planning concept is practicable in each.

The Growing Community. In a locality where rapid and substantial population increase occurs, difficulties frequently arise in relation to school facilities, business services, utilities, recreation, opportunities for religious worship, and other phases of community living. In the Mirage Flats area of northwestern Nebraska, for example, a dry-land farming tract was recently transformed to irrigation agriculture. Where formerly about 23 families had lived, now 110 families were settled, many of which were those of returning G.I.'s who were making up for lost time in getting their families under way. The inhabitants of the Flats found themselves confronted with a whole network of problems demanding prompt solution. The school situation was described in the following excerpt from a report issued by the University of Nebraska:

> Among the major factors in the present educational situation which need to be considered are the following: First, there is the overcrowding apparent in the present school plants. The members of the survey committee visited the school buildings in districts 51, 56, 30, and 125. It was apparent to the survey committee members, and it has already become apparent to members of the Mirage Flats community, that each of these buildings is now housing a number of pupils in excess of reasonable standards. Since in each of these districts a further expansion in enrollment appears to be inevitable, the present buildings are inadequate and may be expected to become increasingly so in the near future.[1]

Situations like these call for careful analysis, for accurate anticipation of future trends, and for continuous planning to meet new needs. This necessity is ordinarily quite clear where

1. Merle A. Stoneman and Otto G. Hoiberg, "The Mirage Flats School District Situation." Unpublished manuscript, November, 1948.

the shoe begins to pinch because of increasing inadequacy of services. It is perhaps here that one finds the greatest readiness to give the community-planning process the attention which it deserves.

The Declining Community. One might expect that people who live in a community which is losing population would see the need for community planning as readily as those who are experiencing rapid growth. This is not true, however, because a greater sense of urgency seems to accompany a scarcity of essential services than an excess thereof.

Notwithstanding, there are many small communities which are prompted by a drop in population, particularly when accompanied by a deteriorating social and economic situation, to examine the concept of community planning as a possible means of stemming the downward trend. Poston has described a number of rural Montana communities, such as Darby, of which this was true.

> Darby was a typical one-street logging town where the clang of silver dollars was heard nightly in local saloons. Most of the inhabitants made their living by cutting trees, or by selling flour and whiskey to the woodsmen. It was a land of wooden gold, for out of Darby's forests thousands of feet of logs moved daily from the lumberjack's saw to the mills of distant cities. But it was a society that could not last, for it was built on the false notion that forests are inexhaustible.
>
> . . . Each succeeding year the lumberjacks cut deeper into the forest. Their absentee employers were not interested in Darby as a community. Their policy, like that which had always dominated the frontier, was strictly cut out and get out. And by 1944, Darby's large private timber holdings had virtually passed into history. It had been another American boom town—settled in a flush of pioneer enthusiasm, boomed to main-street size, and then left to molder and die. . . .
>
> Already there were empty buildings along Main Street, and the town's dilapidated appearance sent strangers hurriedly on their way. Destructive logging had reduced taxable valuation to sixty-

> seven per cent below its 1930 depression level. The support of public education had become critical. Young people graduating from high school found no opportunities in Darby and seventy-five per cent of them were leaving.[2]

Poston goes on to relate how Darby organized a Community Study Group and, through a program of systematic self-analysis, laid the foundation for a promising future.

The Stationary Community. It is in the rural community whose population remains relatively constant that people probably find greatest difficulty in sensing the value of community planning. Lacking is the feeling of urgency which arises where population zooms. The stimulus to forestall disaster from a declining population is also absent. A certain stability prevails from decade to decade which tends to lull people into a sense of complacency.

This is not to imply that serious problems are non-existent in the stationary community. Problems are ordinarily plentiful, but constructive action is more likely to result from a vision of desirable goals that could be attained than from the onslaught of crises that have become acute. There was no crisis in Big Springs, Nebraska,[3] so far as the fine arts were concerned. It was an ordinary small town, with ordinary offerings along cultural lines. But the people wanted something better, and through careful planning and joint action with neighboring small communities, succeeded in establishing a program of concerts and other artistic performances which compares favorably with the offerings of many urban centers.

Community planning is the process whereby a community is transformed most effectively from the kind of place it *is,* into that which it *wants to be*. It promotes the good life in any community, regardless of size or population trend. It repre-

2. Richard Waverly Poston, *Small Town Renaissance* (New York: Harper & Brothers, 1950), pp. 49, 50.
3. See p. 167.

sents the only real alternative to a happy-go-lucky, day-to-day existence and holds real promise for the future of every social group which learns to employ it. Finally, it is in keeping with the best democratic traditions of our American society.

4

COORDINATING COMMUNITY ACTIVITIES

There is nothing more precious than time, and nothing more prodigally wasted.—PROVERB

IT IS OFTEN HELD that life in the small community is simple, quiet, and easygoing. From one standpoint this is true, but in another sense it is certainly a half-truth. Anyone who has lived in a rural community knows that a multiplicity of organizations usually exists, and that an intense, complex pattern of activities often prevails.

Comments like the following are regularly heard in many small towns: "We have every organization known to man!" . . . "Oh, for a night at home! We're on the go continuously" . . . "The proposed get-together sounds good, but it's just impossible to find an open night." . . . "We're sorry that the crowd is so small, Mr. Guest Speaker, but there are three other things going on tonight." . . . "The trouble with this place is that there just aren't enough nights in the week."

Some of these communities conclude that they are "over-organized," which may well be true in the sense that there are too many organizations with similar goals competing for the participation of certain elements of the local population. It may not be true, however, when one considers the possibility that a considerable number of people in that same community may take very meager part in any type of organized group activity at all.

If overorganization of any kind does exist, what can be done to relieve the situation? The most obvious solution would be to eliminate some of the organizations where duplication is evident, but that is a difficult matter indeed! The basic urge for self-preservation which is found in the human being seems also to be characteristic of social organizations. Even where logic points toward the liquidation of a given club, there are feelings of pride, vested interests, or just plain tradition which often prevent it.

At any rate, it is hardly profitable for a community with "too many organizations" to rely entirely upon liquidations or mergers to alleviate the problem. A more immediate and rewarding approach lies in the development of a pattern of coordination among the various groups which will enable each to have a better idea of *what* the others are doing and *when* they plan to do it. This, of course, is a desirable arrangement even where there is not an excessive number of organized groups.

A common device for attaining this goal is the community calendar. It would be a mistake to assume that there is any single arrangement known as the "community calendar." The author has personally observed a considerable variety of arrangements which seem to serve effectively as clearing-houses for the dates of community activities.

In some localities a public-spirited citizen, strategically located, is designated as the central clearing-house for dates. It may be the editor of a local weekly paper, the secretary of a commercial club, or anyone else who is willing, easily accessible, and has the confidence of his fellow citizens. The big difficulty here is usually not in finding a person who meets these specifications, but rather in getting the respective organizations of the community (town and country) into the habit of *using* him as a clearing-house. As one newspaper editor in a town of 1,700 population put it: "I'd be very pleased to provide this central-calendar service, but I just don't have the time to run all over the community pleading with organizations to keep me up-to-date regarding activities which are being planned!" Where common agreement prevails to clear all dates in advance by lifting the telephone receiver or stepping into a centrally located office, this method works exceptionally well. It is simple, direct and informal.

Certain communities go a step further than the procedure just outlined. Instead of merely filing the information with a readily accessible person whom groups can contact in regard to open dates, this person is asked to issue bulletins periodically, listing the dates and events which have been reported to him. It is logical here to make a distinction between regularly recurring events such as the monthly meeting of a Women's Club, on the one hand, and special events such as a church bazaar, on the other. A printed card or calendar listing all the regular events can be circulated to all homes once each year, and mimeographed or dittoed sheets giving advance notice of all special occasions can be posted monthly or at longer intervals in a number of conspicuous places throughout the community, or published in the local paper.

Again, there are localities in which a community council provides, as one of its coordinating services, a calendar of community activities. The community council is an over-all coordinating body on which the various civic-minded groups within any given community are represented. This would normally include most of the organized groups in the town and in the surrounding farm area which belongs to the community. It is not unusual for a rural community to have from twenty to thirty different groups represented on the council, including such as the following: the chamber of commerce, the women's club, the various churches (or a ministerial association), the local Grange, the public school, the village council, and the Home Extension Club. Ordinarily there is a delegate or two from each member organization. Meetings are commonly held quarterly, with provision for extra sessions as need may require.

The problem of determining which organizations can be classified as "civic-minded" must be solved locally in the light of the nature and functions of each organization. No rigid list of eligible organizations can be applied to all communities, because the name of an organization often gives no clue whatever to its essential nature. A Men's Club may be a small group of Saturday-night poker enthusiasts in one locality, and a large public-spirited group dedicated to community development, in another.

The purpose of a community council is to enrich community life by performing certain desirable functions which do not fall within the scope of existing special-interest organizations. One of these, as stated above, is to promote the coordination of community activities by serving as a clearing house for dates and information. The community council is ideally designed to perform this task. Let us assume that at a regular council meeting there are representatives of twenty-five local organizations present. One of the first items on the agenda will be to give each person an opportunity to announce briefly any and all special events that are being planned by his organization during the coming months. Each organization thus lays its cards on the table, and possible conflicts are detected in advance. Even if certain conflicts cannot be averted, the parties concerned will at least be aware of the situation, and this, in itself, is desirable. The information gathered in this manner at each council meeting becomes the basis for a community calendar which thereupon is given as wide a circulation as possible.

Another important function of a community council is to serve as a community forum where all elements of the population can sit down together periodically to discuss local problems of common concern. Group discussion is a commonplace in the small community, but most of it is carried on in casual, informal groupings or within the confines of individual organizations, such as a Chamber of Commerce. For issues which are of interest primarily to the organization concerned, the latter is an acceptable arrangement; but when a problem of community-wide scope is at hand, it becomes desirable to provide for some type of forum where all interests will have an opportunity to be heard. The different points of view will thereby be brought into the open and tested against each other, with possible consensus resulting. Free discussion is an effective means of identifying problem areas, obtaining workable suggestions as to solutions, and welding the members of a group into an integrated whole.

There are many small communities in which no provision whatever is made for common discussion of major issues, no matter how important they may be. The people of the dwindling community to which reference was made on page 5 felt quite uneasy about the downward trend which was in evidence, and yet there had been no occasion during the past decade when its various elements had come together for an objective, diagnostic look at themselves.

One reason for this situation presumably lies in unfortunate past experiences with group discussion techniques. "We tried to get together to discuss this problem, but it just didn't seem to work out. . . . We got off on tangents so much of the time. . . . The usual few did most of the talking. . . . The issues were not clearly defined. . . . The whole business was left hanging in mid-air, with no effort made to summarize what had been said."

There is really no valid reason for this sort of trouble. During recent years, a wealth of excellent materials has been published to guide the layman in leading and participating in effective group discussion. A systematic examination of such materials can contribute much toward making the discussion process more fruitful and meaningful in a community council or anywhere else. Note, for example, the recent bulletin entitled "A Manual for Discussion Leaders and Participants," by Paul Bergevin and Dwight Morris, Community Services in Adult Education, Indiana University. In this inexpensive 73-page pamphlet the layman receives practical information and suggestions as to group discussion methods, physical arrangements, the qualities and attitudes of a good leader, the duties and responsibilities of the leader and the participant, the use of audio-visual and other resource materials, and methods of evaluating group discussion.

A further duty of a community council is to engage in whatever research activities may be desirable in relation to community development proposals under consideration. This is usually done by committees, drawing upon outside resources whenever guidance is needed. The factual data thus gathered lend substance to the discussions noted above and provide helpful information for any group that may subsequently decide to assume responsibility for an action program. A community council which is not afraid to do a little honest-to-goodness digging is more likely to be successful and to gain satisfaction from its work than one which seeks an effortless existence.

Many valuable published aids are available to groups which are interested along this line. Richard W. Poston has written an entire volume[1] designed specifically to help laymen in constructive community self-analysis. Somewhat less elaborate are numerous non-technical check lists or score cards which are well adapted for use in the small community. As an example, the Agricultural Extension Service at Iowa State College has published a series of community rating sheets under the general heading of "Tomorrow's Community," with the following individual units:

Agriculture and Conservation (CDG-3)
Cultural Arts and Recreation (CDG-4)
Education—School and Community (CDG-5)
Government (CDG-6)
Health (CDG-7)
Homes and Family Life (CDG-8)
Industry and Labor (CDG-9)
Religious Life (CDG-10)

1. *Democracy Is You—A Guide to Citizen Action* (New York: Harper & Brothers, 1953).

Whether professionally devised tools such as the above are used or homemade techniques are employed, a study must be thoroughly objective to be meaningful. In many instances a community council can take action on an issue without special research of any kind, but if the latter is required, it should be conducted in an unemotional and unbiased manner. Impartiality is often difficult to maintain where enthusiasm for a cause runs high, but without it, a study becomes a waste of time.

The community council in Ashland, Nebraska, provides a good illustration of how a community council can serve as an agency for community study.[2] There seemed to be general agreement here that a community hall was urgently needed, but rather than jumping headlong into a discussion of fund raising and construction, they proceeded first to gather basic information deemed essential to the success of the proposed project. The community council sent teams to visit other communities where community halls already were in existence, for the purpose of gathering data regarding construction costs, architectural design, and maintenance costs and procedures. In addition, a questionnaire was drawn up and submitted to all organizations which were potential users of the hall. Each group was asked to provide answers to the following questions:

Number of members?
Present meeting place?
How often do you meet? Date? Time of day?
Is your present meeting place adequate?
What was your average attendance last year?
What was your largest attendance at a regular meeting?
What was your largest attendance at a special meeting?
How often would you need to use a community building for special purposes?
What are these typical purposes?
What type of building would best meet your group's needs?
How would you propose paying for and operating such a building?

2. See also p. 26.

Would your group or club help to support a community building by:
  a. Paying a rental fee?
  b. Donations?
  c. Other suggestions?

If facilities were available for dinner meetings, would your group take advantage of them? How often? About how many would be present?

With this and related types of factual information on hand, a sound basis for intelligent action came into being.

A community council which functions effectively as a community forum and which makes careful studies where further data are needed is serving its community well. It has been shown, however, that where these functions are efficiently performed, there is a natural tendency to look next toward an action program. The usual role of a community council is not to develop an action program of its own, but rather to encourage the appropriate agency or combination of agencies to do something about it.

In one small town, for example, the street lights were few in number and all were concentrated on Main Street. Residential areas extending a few blocks in all directions were unlighted except for occasional porch illumination. The ladies in particular were much disturbed at this situation, and after a thorough discussion the community council adopted a resolution calling the matter to the attention of the town board and urging prompt action.

In another instance, a community council pointed up the need for a summer activity program for boys, a project which was promptly initiated by the local American Legion.

In short, a community council is not primarily an action group. Its role is to bring significant problems into focus through its deliberations and to encourage appropriate action by member (or non-member) organizations. It sometimes happens, however, that a need is identified by a community council where the action required is beyond the capacity of any local organization acting alone. A situation of this sort may call for action by the community council itself.

Illustrative of this was Chester, Nebraska (population 539), which prior to 1950 had no park of any kind. The Chester Community Council was cognizant of the need and decided to do something about it. It was felt that the only feasible approach for a project of this magnitude was through direct sponsorship by the Community Council. On Arbor Day a call sent out through all member organizations brought several dozen people from town and country, with tractors, jeeps and strong backs, to help each other transform a number of vacant lots (donated by public-spirited citizens) into a community park. All labor was volunteer. The hedge and 75 trees which were planted were gifts. In a single day most of the work was completed, and Mother Nature is now doing her part to finish a job well started.

Throughout the United States there is probably no type of small community organization which has surpassed the community council in spectacular achievement, on the one hand, and in dismal failure, on the other. Hundreds of instances could be cited where it has been instrumental in marshalling local resources behind outstanding programs of community improvement, but examples of virtual impotence and lifelessness are as readily to be found.

In conclusion, a few words of wisdom which have been culled from the fatality records of community councils are worthy of consideration:

—Every community council (and each committee within it) should grow out of a recognized community need. Don't organize a council or a committee unless it makes sense in your own local setting.

—Your community council should not be permitted to become "just another organization." It is a unique body whose primary purposes are to coordinate diverse efforts, to analyze community needs, and to stimulate community action. Where the sponsorship of special projects is undertaken by the council, this should not be done at the expense of its broader functions.

—Don't permit any single individual or group to dominate the council. It is the *inter-group* agency of your community and should remain such.

—It is desirable for your council to plan a long-term program covering pertinent phases of your community life. However, don't get too many irons into the fire at one time. Start with a job which everyone recognizes as important and do the job right.

—Be sure that both the farm and town elements of your community are fully represented in the council.

—Adequate publicity should be given to the work of the council so that the community may know what is going on. Only in this manner can public interest, so vital to the success of this organization, be maintained.

Communities interested in pursuing this subject further may find the following constitution helpful as a guide.

ARTICLE I

Name

The name of this organization shall be the ________________ Community Council.

ARTICLE II

Purpose

1. It shall promote the coordination of community activities by serving as a clearing house for dates and information.

2. It shall serve as a community forum where representatives of the various groups within the community can discuss local problems of common concern.

3. It shall make such studies as are necessary and feasible.

4. It shall stimulate pertinent local organizations to develop action programs designed to strengthen those areas of community living which are in need of attention.

5. It may sponsor specific community projects itself, but ordinarily only where no existing special-interest group is in position to undertake the work.

ARTICLE III

Membership

1. Each group possessing a civic interest in the community shall be entitled to one representative on the Council. The subsidiary organizations of any given group are normally not eligible for separate representation.

2. A maximum of five additional representatives-at-large may be elected by a majority vote of the Council.

3. The term of membership for representatives shall be one year. Any person who has represented a member organization for three consecutive terms shall be ineligible to represent that organization until one year has elapsed.

4. Disagreement regarding the right of any organization to be represented on the Council shall be settled by majority vote of the Council.

5. Annual dues are payable by each organization represented, the amount to be determined by the Council.

ARTICLE IV

Meetings

1. Regular meetings of the Council shall be held quarterly on the ________________________________.

2. Special meetings of the Council may be called by the Executive Committee upon reasonable notice.

3. The Annual Meeting shall be ________________. At that time the Council representatives and the officers for the coming year shall take office.

ARTICLE V

Officers

1. At the Annual Meeting each year the following officers shall be elected from the membership of the Council:

a. A president who shall preside at the Council meetings.

b. A vice-president who shall preside in the absence of the president.

c. A secretary-treasurer who shall keep an official record of all proceedings of the Council, handle all funds in a manner authorized by the Council, and perform such additional functions as normally pertain to this office.

ARTICLE VI

Committees

1. The Executive Committee shall consist of the president, vice-president, and secretary-treasurer of the Council. Its function is to assure that the decisions of the Council are properly carried out.

2. Additional committees shall be appointed by the Council to deal with those areas of community life in which recognized needs exist.

ARTICLE VII

Amendment

This constitution may be amended by majority vote at any regular meeting of the Council, provided each member organization has received one month's written notice stating that the proposed amendment is to be considered.

In concluding this chapter on coordinating community activities, it should be noted that the devices which have been described are only illustrative of the many which are in effective use. There are numerous ways of attaining the desired goal, and whatever works well in one locality may not be suitable in another. Each community will seek out the method, formal or informal, which serves its purpose best.

5

DIMINISHING SOCIAL CLEAVAGES

I don't like that person—I must get to know him better.
—ABRAHAM LINCOLN

SERIOUS INTERNAL DISSENSION is a luxury which the small community can ill afford, particularly if it is of an abiding nature. Civic improvement programs are to a large extent dependent upon voluntary joint effort in rural areas, and such effort is marred by cleavages among local groups.

In every community there is room for diversity of viewpoints on both major and minor issues. In fact, the absence of vigorous differences of opinion and opposing "schools of thought" is likely to be a sign of stagnation. It is through consensus derived from such diversity that progress becomes possible. This is the American way.

The difficulty does not lie in the differences in viewpoint themselves, because even the greatest of these can eventually be resolved if a desire for consensus exists. The almost insurmountable conflict between the large states and the small states at the Constitutional Convention in 1787, for instance, could have ended in stalemate and failure, but the Convention leaders were statesmen with a will to solve this problem. An acceptable solution was found in a two-house arrangement for Congress.

The magnitude of the differences in the small community are thus of far less significance than the basic orientation of the individuals or groups concerned toward each other and toward their community and its problems. A precarious situation exists when they lose sight of the fact that they stand on common ground. At that point, normal communication among the various elements breaks down because minds begin to close and the possibility of cooperative action toward community goals wanes. Instead of one community, there may actually be two, each living in social isolation of the other or actually working at cross-purposes to it.

A case in point is a small hamlet where a personal feud between two leading citizens had caused the entire community to split into two camps, neither of which would have anything to do with the other. An outsider's suggestion that the two warring factions might possibly re-establish working relations by getting together on a Christmas program for the youngsters of the community was met with the retort: "I doubt we could sit down together to plan even that project without flying at each other's throats!" This kind of situation may be good for people who enjoy conflict, but it is hardly conducive to community progress.

Cleavages in the small community may take many forms. Among the most common are those which have to do with town-country relations, age groups, social class, and population mobility. Each of these will be considered in turn.

In many parts of the world today there is no town-and-country problem, because the farmers live in villages as part of the "village community." G.I.'s who were stationed in Bavaria after World War II observed the complete absence of farm buildings in the open country. Picturesque towns house not only the merchants and other villagers (as we use this term), but also the people who till the soil adjoining the population center. All live together as a social unit, and while this does not eliminate the possibility of cleavage between the farm and non-farm elements, at least the distance factor does not exist. Daily personal contacts provide an excellent opportunity for them to become well acquainted with each other as individuals, and this is important where integration is desired.

This very arrangement characterized much of early New England in our own country and still prevails there in certain areas. The Mormons likewise have used it. But the most common pattern of settlement in the United States has become the town-and-country arrangement, where the farm families live alone and in scattered fashion on the agricultural lands surrounding the village.

This pattern has certain advantages. It brings the farm family close to the earth which they till and thereby encourages a more intense love of the land than could be expected if they lived in a village and commuted daily to their fields. Their land becomes *home* to them, not merely a source of income.

Among the drawbacks, however, is a danger that social barriers will arise between villagers and the farm population. As was pointed out in Chapter 1, the rural community in most parts of our nation comprises farmers and townspeople living in a given geographical area and bound together by vital common interests and by a sense of belonging. Unfortunately the feeling of community is incomplete in many instances. As one farmer put it: "We farmers feel that a sort of wall exists between you folks in town and us farmers!" At times there is open hostility between town and country, but usually the cleavage finds a somewhat more subtle expression in the social relationships between farmer and villager.

Witness, for example, the new community club which had just been organized in a certain rural locality, with the farm element even more strongly represented than the village. The nominating committee was in closed session to draw up the first slate of officers. At the suggestion that a certain young farmer of unquestioned leadership ability be considered for president, one highly respected member of the committee hesitatingly said, "I realize that the farmers are a vital part of our community, but somehow I feel that we should keep the leadership of the community club here in town." This man was in no way antagonistic toward the farmers and recognized them as members of the community, but apparently not on a fully equal footing with the village residents.

In another instance the farmers were excluded from a men's club in town because "they go to neighboring towns for so many of their purchases." To which the farmers' reply was: "Well, if that's the way they feel about it, we *will* go to other places to do our trading!"

This problem is more important than it often seems, and there is no point in blaming any particular group, because it is ordinarily a two-way proposition. In any given situation it is advisable for everyone concerned—farmer and town resident alike—to re-examine carefully his innermost thoughts and feelings on the subject.

The community which is confronted with a cleavage of this nature may find the following suggestions helpful. First, be sure that there is adequate representation of both the farm and town elements in any organization or project which is of community-wide proportions. There is probably no more effective means of strengthening human bonds than working together toward the attainment of a common goal. If it is to be a community activity, it should become so in fact as well as on paper.

Second, study the "sore spots" in your farm-town relationships and try to do something about them. Among the more prevalent sources of irritation to the farm population are the day-long monopolizing of Saturday parking spaces in the business district by merchants and other town residents, frequently making it necessary for farmers to carry heavy loads of groceries to their cars parked in outlying areas, and the lack of adequate restroom facilities in town for farm women and children.

Third, get together socially in both formal and informal activities. A friendly visit and a good time together can go a long way toward building mutual respect and confidence. Among the many types of gatherings which have proved effective are community dinners honoring 4-H Club members; Christmas parties with treats for all youngsters; weekly evening band concerts or other entertainment throughout the summer months; films, lectures, and other programs suited to the tastes of both farmers and townspeople; and community-wide celebrations built around cultural characteristics or historical events which are distinctive of the community.

Incidentally, there is good reason to believe that the problem of town-and-farm cleavage is becoming less serious as time goes on. Rural sociologists point out that the village is increasingly becoming a center for the social activities of the entire community. With modern transportation facilities and good roads available, many farmers are now sending their youngsters to school in town rather than in the open-country; numerous outlying churches are closing their doors in favor of places of worship in the village; and recreational opportunities are being sought in municipalities to a much greater degree than was formerly true. In short, the farmers are now going to town for more and more of their activities, and in so doing, they mingle more closely and frequently with their village brethren. A higher degree of identification between the two groups therefore becomes possible.

While a natural trend may thus exist toward the elimination of town-and-country cleavage, the same probably cannot be said of that between the younger and older generations within the community. There are, in fact, grounds for assuming that problems in this area may become more acute. The proportion of our total population which is 65 years of age or older has risen from 2.6 per cent in 1850 to more than 8 per cent at the present time. Against an increase of about 20 per cent in total U. S. population since 1940, this age group has grown by nearly

50 per cent, comprising now about 13.5 million people.[1] The older element of our population, in other words, is growing relatively more powerful as time goes on. This development is of no mean interest to the small town, because it already has a disproportionate share of the aged among its residents.

We do not mean to imply that the pattern of relationships between the generations is predominantly one of conflict and dissension. Nor do we feel that there is invariably a positive correlation between advanced chronological age and conservatism. Nevertheless, as the following illustration suggests, there is ample justification for our reference to cleavage in this connection.

In a certain village, the younger element had for years attempted to obtain sewerage facilities for the town. Consistently the older, retired citizens had blocked their efforts by coming out in strength at election time to vote the recurring proposal down. Now, however, the goal had been reached. Sewer tiles were lying along the streets, and the digging apparatus was poised for action. Upon being asked why the bond election finally had carried after so many failures, a local booster replied: "Well, sir, the reason is not far to seek! We have a very substantial group of retired individuals in this town who buck practically everything that costs a little money. The demand of our younger folks for flush toilets has always been met with the remark that 'We've gotten along O.K. all these years with outdoor privies, so why should we spend a lot of money now for anything else?' "

"There was particularly one old man," the informant continued, "who had been a ringleader in this regard. During the weeks just prior to a bond election he would make the rounds among all the old folks and campaign against the proposed sewer system. This time, however, one of our outstanding young men went to the old man and had a long heart-to-heart talk

1. *Statistical Bulletin,* Metropolitan Life Insurance Company (New York, December, 1953), p. 2.

with him. It was tactfully suggested that in his waning years he might wish to support at least this one progressive proposal which was so strongly desired by his younger fellow citizens. Whatever may have happened, the old gentleman had a change of heart, and that's why you see these tiles on the street before you now."

It is difficult to find an effective means of resolving the lack of rapport between a younger generation with its eyes on the future, and an older generation which thinks largely in terms of maintaining the status quo. Such cleavage is as old as human society itself, but this gives small comfort to the enterprising young adult who wants to see his own particular generation contribute its full measure of progress in the life of his community. In relation to any project on which the generations stand opposed, it may be helpful to keep the following guideposts in mind.

First, it should be recognized that each party to the struggle usually has valid and understandable reasons for its viewpoint. An honest effort to appreciate the other fellow's position on the issue would seem to be an essential foundation for any progress toward agreement.

Second, there is little to be gained by personal attacks upon the opposition. This ordinarily leads to a negative, uncompromising, and retaliatory frame of mind—which leads nowhere.

Third, the most effective approach appears to be through friendly, open-minded conversation, primarily with the natural leaders of the opposing side. These natural leaders are not difficult to identify in the small community. They are extremely important in molding community opinion on any issue, and every effort should be made to help them "see the light."

Fourth, it is advisable to assemble all pertinent factual information and publicize it widely. Many an elderly citizen has voted against a new community hall or other civic improvement largely because of ill-founded (and sometimes maliciously planted) rumors that confiscatory tax rates would result. It is an easy matter to calculate accurately the increase in taxes on old Mrs. Smith's house which will result from the bond issue proposed. She has a right to know exactly what the effect will be, and she can be expected to oppose the project until she *does* know. Often the "obstinacy" of the retired citizens stems from a fear that the proposed development would constitute a threat to their economic security, and if they can be shown that their fear is without substance, they may well experience a change of heart.

Finally, it is sometimes possible to attain the goal by doing a little "horse trading." This course of action is undesirable where it leads a person to vote for something which he fundamentally opposes in order to obtain something for himself. It is an acceptable and practicable procedure, however, when it involves giving your opponent a hand in relation to a socially desirable objective which he may have, in return for which he becomes more favorably inclined toward the program which you have in mind.

A further type of cleavage is apparent in what sociologists call social stratification. This has reference to the tendency of social groups to divide themselves into classes or castes, arranged above or below each other according to some extra-legal rating device.

We Americans have been hesitant to admit that stratification does, in fact, exist in our land. All the while we have known that it does. Concrete evidence thereof is not difficult to find, regardless of where one may be. *Here,* for instance, is a modern attractive restaurant displaying a sign "Indian trade not solicited" which somewhat less than tactfully reminds the original American that he is a second-rate human being in the social system of today. *There* is a harmless-looking sign stating that "we reserve the right to refuse service to anyone," which ostensibly refers to drunks and their kind, but actually serves notice on Negroes, Mexicans or others of minority group status that they are not considered fit company for people of white skin. *Over yonder* is an unwritten arrangement which bars young Mr. Goldberg from enrolling in Quota College because he is a Jew. Only so many of his kind are permitted to enter, and no more.

Such evidences of social class and caste in the United States are obvious, even to the casual observer. They represent a social cleavage, whether found in urban or rural areas, which greatly hampers the democratic functioning of our social institutions. Alert citizens everywhere are aware of this and progress is being made on many fronts, but the road ahead is still long and arduous. Most forms of social stratification are somewhat less clear-cut than those alluded to above. Numerous studies have been made in recent years by social scientists which throw light upon social classes in the rural community.

The research work done by Earl H. Bell in a small Iowa community, Shell Rock, revealed a class structure comprising five social strata, which faded imperceptibly into each other. The social classes delineated were hardly recognized as such by local residents, but they existed nevertheless. The lowest class consisted of farm laborers and others who worked on a more or less casual basis. Above these were the tenant farmers, some of whom were identified with the laborers but others of whom approached the next higher class, the farmer-owner, in the social ladder. Above the land-owning farmers came the business and professional people in town who, in turn, were topped by the banker and a small group of his associates.

A small Missouri town fictitiously called Plainville was investigated by James West, who found evidence of three social strata: "upper class," "good lower class people," and the "lower element."[2] Further, a great deal of scientific evidence on social stratification has been gathered from the Cotton Belt to verify the popularly recognized social classes which lie between the

2. James West, *Plainville, U.S.A.* (New York: Columbia University Press, 1945).

"poor white trash" at the bottom, and the Southern aristocracy at the top.

The reader who is interested in sociological studies of this nature will find an excellent summary in *Rural Social Systems,* by Charles P. Loomis and J. Allan Beegle. But it is hardly necessary to examine scientific studies for evidences of social stratification. Almost every community will reveal such cleavage in some degree or other to anyone who looks objectively for it. In one good-sized middle-western rural community, for instance, a substantial recreation program for youth had been conducted for several years, but for some reason the "kids from the other side of the tracks" consistently failed to participate. The official welcome mat was certainly out to *all* children of the community, but apparently the "wrong-side" youngsters did not feel wanted or at ease with those from the "better" part of town, and so they took no part in the organized recreational program.

Similarly, a social worker who had lived for a number of years in a small county seat stated that "the people living in the upper part of town" rarely had anything to do in a social way with the others. The former were not snobbish or antagonistic; they simply did not associate with fellow citizens unless they lived in the "right" part of town.

The extent of class consciousness in the rural community can easily be exaggerated, but to the extent that this phenomenon does exist, it should be recognized and evaluated in the light of general community welfare. What can be done about it?

Differences in economic status, pattern of living, and social prestige exist everywhere, and ordinarily these are significant factors in determining the people with whom one associates. The local doctor or banker is more likely to associate with other professional or business persons than with the clerk or farm laborer, and vice versa. Such groupings are, of course, perfectly natural, since people tend to select their friends and associates on the basis of common interests.

If serious cleavage exists, it is time for careful thinking. We Americans have always taken pride in the fact that our social classes tend to be indistinct and that an opportunity to rise exists for anyone who has the necessary ability and energy. It is up to the individual community to assure that such conditions prevail as will make this possible.

Some rural communities have attempted to counteract social stratification by planning projects or programs which require the cooperation of all classes within the community. This approach is based on the assumption that joint activity creates better understanding among diverse groups, and that better understanding tends to soften class lines. In addition to participating fully in broad cooperative programs, everyone would do well to make a specific point of establishing personal acquaintance with as many people as possible in the social classes or minority groups that lie "below" him on the social scale. We tend to think of such groups in terms of broad generalities, social stereotypes, labelling all individuals included as having similar characteristics. The fallacy of such thinking can often be brought to light through personal acquaintance with members of the group concerned.

As a guidepost in relation to this problem, one can turn to our Preamble statement that "all men are created equal . . ." A genuine re-dedication to this truth will contribute much toward keeping class consciousness in its appropriate place of subordinance to community consciousness.

Throughout our history we have been a mobile people, and our mobility has taken many forms. In a gigantic and colorful westward movement, our entire country was occupied. A long-term cityward trend has transformed a rural nation into one that today is nearly two-thirds urban. During the five-year period from 1935 to 1940, 12.5 per cent of all people over five years of age moved across county lines.[3] Thousands of migra-

3. Kolb and Brunner, *op. cit.*, p. 27.

tory workers make their annual treks with the harvests in beet field and orchard. The years of World War II gave rise to great migrations of labor to and from defense plants throughout the country.

High mobility, of whatever type it may be, tends to counteract the development of a feeling of community which characterizes more stable populations, and marked cleavages may result. People who are "here today and gone tomorrow" ordinarily do not sink roots, and roots are essential to identification with any community.

Rural sociologists have long been concerned about high tenancy rates, partly because farm tenants move several times more often than do farm owners. Social institutions suffer from excessive mobility of people, and a sustained, well-integrated effort toward community improvement becomes difficult.

One of the most spectacular illustrations of population mobility was that which characterized the many defense areas which sprang up throughout the nation during the recent war period. The author had occasion to study in some detail a few of the sociological problems resulting from the establishment of the Nebraska Ordnance Plant at Mead, a small town of 260 people. Among these problems was the cleavage between the permanent residents of Mead and those who came in temporarily for the period of plant construction.

From its founding in 1877 until the erection of the Nebraska Ordnance Plant in 1942, Mead was a peaceful little village surrounded by fertile, level agricultural lands. In general outward appearance it was a typical small town, with its two-block business district and a residential area of 112 homes. Its population of 324 in 1890 had dropped to 260 by 1940, and nothing had happened throughout its entire history to disturb its quietude, save possibly the establishment and brief operation of a ballast factory by the Union Pacific Railroad late in the nineteenth century.

Then the federal government decided to construct a $25,-

000,000 bomb-loading plant virtually in the back yard of Mead, a project which temporarily brought up to 9,000 construction workers to that vicinity. The population of Mead itself swelled to almost 2,000. The usually deserted business district of Mead was jammed with endless rows of tightly parked cars 24 hours a day, and the streets and sidewalks were crowded to overflowing. A village official stated that it was not uncommon to see 600 men waiting in line before the employment office on Main Street. Trailers came to town in swarms and at the peak of the construction period outnumbered the permanent village residences by more than two to one.

Extreme mobility characterized the newcomers in the Mead community. The local school superintendent reported: "I took the school census during the construction boom and it's one of the worst headaches I've ever had! Family 'A' was in this house today; in another two days later; and then gone altogether from the community! I don't believe I knew much more after I finished that census than I did before I started."

As far as the permanent residents of the area were concerned, one of the regrettable aspects of this situation proved to be the failure of the construction workers to identify themselves in any way with their new, though temporary, community. They revealed a decided lack of interest in church and other community activities. As one of the clergymen put it, "We did everything we could to interest these workers in our church activities, but it was not much use. Most of them were migratory, just moving from one construction job to the next. They were distinctly a temporary group."

Interviews with families of construction workers who had come to Mead from other communities indicated that in a large majority of the cases their level of participation in organized community activities had fallen sharply upon arrival here. Most of these families stated that this was a purely voluntary decision on their part and attributed their failure to enter into the organized social life of the community to such reasons as the following: "We just want a rest." "We haven't been roped in yet." "My wife had a nervous breakdown before we moved, and we've decided to cut down on activities." "There's nothing to do in Mead but go to church, and we don't care for that."

This illustration is extreme, but it symbolizes the tendency of mobility to discourage identification with established community groups. The higher the degree of mobility, the more difficult the problem of identification becomes and the more serious the cleavage between permanent and temporary residents is apt to be.

Perhaps the most logical approach to the problem of integrating a mobile population, of whatever type, into fuller group living is to study as carefully as possible the causes of mobility within the community. Of further interest, of course, is the specific relation which exists between mobility and the degree of participation in local community activities. In most states assistance in making such studies is readily available from the state university or from other institutions of higher learning.

This research will throw light upon the nature and extent of the problem and enable the community to take such remedial measures as may be appropriate. Where the causes of excessive mobility are beyond the power of the community to control, and they often are, reliance will have to be placed upon a concerted effort to encourage all newcomers to feel at home as rapidly as possible. This can be done by friendly personal contacts through the churches, business firms, civic organizations and other local institutions. Best of all, however, is the informal neighborly chat which perhaps does more than anything else to break down the barriers of unfamiliarity.

The problem of integrating the newcomer may seem irrelevant to rural communities, but an honest soul searching is generally in order. Some have developed a certain smugness over the years, often unknown to themselves, which makes them regrettably well satisfied with their social groupings just as they are. Anybody new who tends to disturb the routine or balance is subconsciously or openly resented and finds difficulty in becoming accepted. This is particularly true where a given religious denomination or nationality tends to be dominant or where cliques play an important role. In such communities it is difficult, even for newcomers who plan permanent residence, to acquire the feeling that they *belong*. In the case of the more or less temporary residents, many of whom are personally inclined toward remaining on the sidelines, the problem becomes even more acute. The new resident, temporary or permanent, needs a community and the community needs him.

6

LEADERSHIP DEVELOPMENT

It is better to light a candle than to curse the darkness.—PROVERB

MUCH OF THE CIVIC IMPROVEMENT WORK done in the small community is of a volunteer nature, as has been pointed out above. If a community hall is to be constructed, it may be done entirely with public funds, but more likely than not it will involve voluntary contributions or volunteer labor in some degree. If a conspicuous public area in town is to be cleaned up and landscaped, the local Garden Club enthusiasts will probably be the ones to do it. If a village park is to be planned, built and adequately equipped, the voluntary groups of the community are almost certain to be involved in some way or other. From one standpoint this is a handicap to the small community, and yet these cooperative ventures provide rural people with repeated opportunities to strengthen community integration in a manner that is quite unknown in urban settings.

There are some experiences that a person never forgets. Early in the writer's career he spent seven years in Askov, a small village nestled in the wild birch, pine and deer country of northern Minnesota. During that winter of winters, 1935-36, this small community was snowed in as seldom before, and the narrow township feeder roads were blocked to the point where only sleighs could pass. Eventually the heavens relaxed, giving the county road equipment a chance to plow out some of the minor roads. But these Askov roads were plugged to the extent that the huge snowplow was helpless—unless manpower could be obtained to shovel away the snow after each plunge or two forward.

There was neither money nor inclination to hire the large shovelling crew that would be needed; so the pattern of volunteer activity perfected through the years went into action. Calls were placed to strategic individuals in the community: "All able-bodied men report at the parsonage at 9 P.M. with snow shovels!"

At the designated hour they were ready: preacher, teacher, farmer, printer, merchant, trucker, day-laborer, mechanic, and all the others. A group of twenty-five enthusiastic men worked with cheer and vigor throughout the entire night, breaking the packed snow before the advancing plow. The labors were punctuated with periodic coffee breaks, wisecracks, practical jokes, and by the hilarious swan-dive of a jolly, rotund music teacher who got too close to the plunging plow and landed in the ditch 'mid an avalanche of snow.

By sunrise the roads were cleared and the men turned to their regular duties, tired but enriched by the fellowship which they had enjoyed while the world around them slept.

Experiences of this nature recur in many phases of small community activity and constitute one of the genuine assets of rural living. But it is precisely this fact that places such a premium on leadership. Without good leaders, these voluntary activities simply fail to materialize.

Rural communities differ widely in the strength of leadership which is in evidence. In some localities there are leaders on hand for almost every type of activity that is undertaken, and things always seem to "click." In others, one desirable project after another fails to develop beyond the discussion stage because "we just don't have the leaders!" While it would be unrealistic to minimize these differences, it must be emphasized that fundamentally they may not be as great as they seem. Perhaps the explanation lies not so much in the presence or absence of leadership talent within the community as in the community's success or failure in bringing the talent to light. Leadership does not operate in a vacuum. It blossoms only where a group situation prevails which enables it to develop and mature. There are many small communities which lack leaders, not because of any actual scarcity of leadership talent but because their social climates are such as to make its realization exceedingly difficult.

This unfavorable social climate is not easily described, but let us try to note a few of its more common manifestations. First, there is the belief that all real leaders are *born* leaders. On the surface, this may not be recognized as a deterrent to leadership development, but in a deeper sense it is exactly that. A community in which this belief is generally held will wait longingly for these biological wonders, the born leaders, to appear, and when they do not, will settle back into a passive acceptance of a fate that has been unkind to them. It is probably not unfair to say that this philosophy is sometimes merely the rationalization of a community's lethargy or lack of confidence in itself. The people do not have the initiative to seek out and develop leaders within their own group, or they suffer from a feeling of inadequacy and therefore retreat to the comforting thought that leadership qualities arise from certain exceptional combinations of genes which are not subject to control in human society. They themselves certainly cannot be held responsible for the unfortunate situation!

The weakness of this attitude becomes apparent when one examines the leadership structure of small communities which are known to be dynamic. To illustrate: Grange No. 371 of Township "K," Seward County, Nebraska, won a $15,000 national first prize for outstanding community service in 1951, having placed seventh, fourth, and second, respectively, in the three foregoing years. It is conceivable that this small rural community (population of hamlet, 67) has been blessed with an exceptional array of "born leaders" who became instrumental in developing the splendid program of community projects which won nationwide acclaim. Examination revealed a far greater likelihood that the Goehner Grange members were ordinary rural Americans, differing from many others primarily in the strength of their devotion to the cause of community development, in the extent to which they had learned the art of working together, and in an unswerving confidence in their ability to produce their own leaders.

The secret of community leadership lies not so much in finding a few outstanding persons who have the knack of making things happen, as it does in the development of a pattern of cooperative effort in which the leadership talents of every member of the group find opportunity for expression. For it is true in a very literal sense that everyone has leadership qualities of one type or another.

This leads us to the second common obstacle to leadership development: the notion that the real leader is necessarily an over-all leader, the sort of individual who can give sturdy and enlightened guidance to his community in almost any situation.

The fallacy of this line of thought can be shown by a casual check of the leaders of virtually any community. Most of them will in all probability be people whose abilities are confined to several distinct areas and who are like fish out of water when asked to serve in other capacities. A business leader may have very little to offer as baseball coach for the Midgets, as choir director in his church, as master of ceremonies on festive occasions, as parliamentarian, or in a variety of other activities calling for special types of leadership talent. Those who have outstanding abilities along many lines die young in the rural community (unless they learn occasionally to say *no*), leaving the work to fellow citizens with capacities of more limited scope. It is important that every person be regarded as a potential leader and that constant effort be made to recognize and cultivate the widely distributed leadership traits which exist.

One of the finest Cub Scout leaders known to the writer was not "discovered" in his community until he was a middle-aged man. Quite by accident he was invited to participate in a minor phase of Cub activities, and within one year he became a strong and respected leader of the entire program. Even he himself was not aware of his ability to work with young boys until this opportunity came along and opened a new and stimulating world to him.

In another instance a woman who had never thought of herself as possessing any particular artistic talent enrolled in a short course where various types of handicrafts were taught. She was fascinated with the things she learned, and before long had developed a major hobby interest. Her work was obviously of such quality that she was soon called upon to teach copper tooling, leathercraft and similar activities in her own community, where she today occupies a place of unquestioned leadership.

One cannot help wondering how much hidden talent of this nature exists in a community which complains about its lack of leaders. A constructive step that has been taken in some localities is to develop a careful inventory of special interests and abilities, based on brief questionnaires filled out by the local residents. Detailed references to this technique as applied to recreation and education are made in Chapters 8 and 9.[1] There is a common tendency in rural areas to assume that everyone knows everything about everybody, but this appears to be somewhat exaggerated. Much helpful information has come to light through systematic checks, even in diminutive hamlet-centered communities.

Coupled with a continuing search for leadership ability in all its various forms should be an earnest effort to afford people of limited experience an opportunity to obtain more experience.

1. See pp. 95, 102-104.

This helps them to mature, and the leadership resources of the community will grow accordingly.

But here a third stumbling block sometimes appears, in the form of an "aristocracy of leadership" which holds a vested interest in positions of authority and influence. This obstacle may take the form of a highly capable individual who serves alone in his special leadership capacity through the years and acquires an aura of indispensability. Despite the valuable service rendered by a leader of this type, his monopolistic position tends to forestall the development of other leaders who ordinarily would appear on the scene when leadership responsibilities are assigned from time to time. Another drawback lies in the tendency of such a leader to retain his key post after his real effectiveness has long since begun to wane.

Sometimes responsibility for this situation lies with the perennial leader himself, but frequently the entire community is at fault for permitting itself to develop an emotional attachment to a single leader, at the expense of other potential resources, or for sliding into the "indispensable man" rut which so often ends in a void.

Another common form of this aristocracy is found in groups of people who over the years retain their positions of control with an iron grip, excluding all others from the inner circle. Such an instance came to light in conversation with a young superintendent of schools some years ago in a small village. He feared for the future of his community, he said, because the young adults were showing less and less interest in its affairs. "And I'll tell you why!" he added. "The old folks have been in the saddle for years around here—on the school board, on the various church boards, and in all positions of importance in our civic and social organizations. When it comes to decision-making, we younger folks are simply excluded. I don't know what the reason for this is—selfishness, short-sightedness, mistrust of the younger generation, or what—but of this I am certain: the whole thing is going to backfire in terms of the long-run welfare of this community. Already the younger element is slowly drifting out of organized community activities, and by the time the oldsters become too feeble to carry on, there won't be anyone here who is interested in taking over!"

This problem can sometimes be alleviated by educational efforts, stressing continuous development of new leadership resources as essential to the future welfare of the community. An alternative approach is a concerted effort by the younger group to vote their representatives into office.

A final hindrance to the emergence of leaders lies in the petty jealousies which so often blemish life in the small community. These exist also in urban society but perhaps loom larger in rural areas because relationships there are so informal and personal. Too often a qualified person turns down an important community responsibility because he has learned from bitter experience that it is a "thankless job." It is not uncommon for a person who has accepted a post with the best of intentions to be accused of all sorts of base motives: He's a publicity seeker! . . . All he's after is the financial gain it will bring him! . . . It's his ambitious wife who pushed him into it! . . . He took the job just to keep my friend from getting it! . . . He has no intention whatever of doing anything—just watch him sit on it till it dies! . . . He's got something up his sleeve!

And then there are the eternal gripers who make life miserable for anyone who has courage enough to take the lead. Many leaders are calloused to this kind of talk and pay little attention to it. But there are others, more sensitive in nature, who take such criticism to heart and become discouraged to the point of withdrawing from the scene. Certainly this is true of many capable men who have served as local governmental officials, and it is by no means confined to the field of politics.

There are a few scoundrels who misuse their positions of influence in the community for selfish ends, but the very fact that our democratic society continues to grow in stature seems to indicate that most leaders are reasonably honest and capable. It behooves the citizens of local communities to avoid unfair criticism and small talk, both of which tend to discourage the very type of unselfish leadership which they so sorely need.

In summary, then, the rural community which allegedly suffers from a lack of leaders can probably relieve the situation appreciably over a period of time by adopting a working philosophy which holds that leaders are *made,* not born, that most leadership talent is of a specialized nature, that a conscious effort must be made to cultivate and utilize latent resources if they are to materialize, and finally, that good leaders can most readily be encouraged to serve in an atmosphere of wholesome maturity in the community.

Many excellent books, pamphlets and articles have been written on the philosophy of leadership, and others deal primarily with techniques. Both aspects are significant, and every rural leader will find his tasks simpler and more enjoyable if he takes the trouble to do a little reading on the subject.

Among the most helpful publications to appear in recent years is *Adult Leadership,* the official organ of the Adult Education Association of the U.S.A.[2] This periodical is written authoritatively in non-academic language and regularly presents helpful suggestions on a wide variety of problems which are troublesome to community leaders. In addition, it is of real assistance to lay leaders who wish to understand more fully their own roles in relation to the groups of which they are a part.

In conclusion, let us consider briefly two weaknesses which frequently mar the effectiveness of the local leader. The first of these is lack of confidence in one's ability to do the job. Without question there are many potential leaders who never advance beyond the potential stage because they lack the courage to step into positions of leadership which, on the surface, appear to require know-how beyond their present capacities. Likewise,

2. See also pp. 110-111.

there are many already in positions of leadership whose work is below par because they are "scared to death." In some instances this lack of self-confidence is a temporary phenomenon which disappears with experience at the helm. In others, there is a real need for further training before the person becomes capable of performing the task at hand.

Rural communities should take note of the many types of leadership training which are available to their citizens. Prominent among these are various types of literature, as indicated above; short courses and institutes, as exemplified by the leadership training programs sponsored by Purdue and Indiana universities through their office of Community Services in Adult Education; conferences and conventions, many of which provide excellent training opportunities; correspondence courses in subjects such as parliamentary law; and local study groups designed to develop leadership skills.

A second ailment which often minimizes the effectiveness of local leaders is the unfortunate urge to assume leadership roles as ends in themselves. Some people have "an itch for leadership," as Arthur E. Morgan has aptly expressed it.[3] Such leaders have the wrong philosophy. Their chief interest is to be in the limelight or to feel the thrill of power. They strive toward entrenching themselves rather than toward helping their groups mature to the point where their leadership functions are no longer necessary. Service to their fellow men is an incidental motive.

It is wholesome for every person entrusted with leadership responsibility to ponder occasionally the fact that *service* and *humility* were dominant in the life of the greatest Leader known to man. The principles of genuine leadership have not changed since that day. Any contemporary leader who deviates from them will find help in a lonely walk under a starlit sky and in an objective evaluation of himself in the light of what he sees.

3. Arthur E. Morgan, *The Small Community* (New York: Harper & Brothers, 1942), p. 170.

PART TWO

PROBLEM AREAS

7

BUSINESS AND INDUSTRY

Great opportunities come to all, but many do not know that they have met them.—DUNNING

EVERY TOWN-CENTERED RURAL COMMUNITY provides economic services of various kinds for its people. In the smallest places such services may be confined to a grocery store and a filling station, but in the larger villages it is not uncommon to find a complex network of economic activities.

The importance of a sound economic base for the community can hardly be overemphasized. It is essential to the successful operation of other social institutions and determines in considerable measure the breadth and depth of the community activities which are possible. A low income level among the farmers and businessmen of a community will ordinarily be reflected in the quality of its schools, churches, and in its program of civic affairs as a whole.

Some time ago a rural pastor was showing the author a stretch of farm land along the Nebraska side of the Missouri River. The land was hilly, and erosion was taking a heavy toll on farms where conservation practices had not been initiated. Upon entering a small town where he served a congregation on a part-time basis, we noted that the entire village bore unmistakable marks of decadence. Store fronts were unpainted, the gaunt stare of vacant buildings was everywhere in evidence, the residences had long since seen their most attractive days, and streets begged for attention. "This used to be a nice little town," said the pastor, "but, as you can see, it is really on the skids now. The reason is that the farmers hereabouts have been very slow to adopt erosion control and other soil conservation practices. So we've been losing our good topsoil and are now trying to make a living off poorer soil. This means that our farmers are having a rougher time of it financially, which, in turn, affects our merchants adversely, and leads to a general decline in community strength and activity."

On the other hand, it must not be assumed that a favorable economic situation necessarily leads to a high type of community living, any more than individual wealth automatically results in a superior quality of personal living. The economic base is essentially a permissive or limiting factor which makes certain things possible, and others not, in a given community. The use to which the available resources are put will be determined by the vision, ingenuity and energy of the people.

Determining Services to Be Offered

One of the more difficult problems confronting the small town in its quest for economic strength is that of determining what services it should endeavor to provide for the people of its trade area. As the head of the Community Club in a town of about 1,000 put it: "We are 40 miles from a city of a quarter million on one side and 30 miles from a city of a hundred thousand on the other. Both are growing rapidly and our merchants are becoming more and more uncertain and confused as to just which economic services our little town should try to provide. We know that our people will trade here for their groceries, and we are equally certain that they will not trade here for their Sunday-go-to-meeting clothes; but there are many types of products regarding which the picture is not so clear. Everything we do must be done with one eye on these neighboring cities, and we are having trouble in deciding just what we can and can't do under the circumstances!"

A similar problem was reflected in another village, population about 800, which felt that it was losing too much business from its logical trade area to neighboring villages and small cities. In an effort to gain clarification as to why this was so, a study was made. The findings pointed up certain gaps in the economic services provided by the village—gaps which were known to exist, to be sure, but whose significance in the total trade pattern was not fully realized. The weaknesses noted in retail trade lines "appeared especially in farm implements, shoes, and men's furnishings and suits."[1]

It was recognized that a weakness in any essential retail line might well lead to a loss of business, not only in that specific line but in others as well. A farmer who finds it necessary to go to a neighboring town for the servicing of his farm machinery, for instance, will often purchase groceries, work clothes, and other things while he is there.

The Chamber of Commerce in this community thereupon held a series of meetings to study their findings and to map procedures for eventually providing the deficient services which were considered essential to the economic well-being of the community as a whole.

Historical perspective is quite important for the small trade center which is attempting to determine its logical role in the broad, complex, and constantly changing pattern of economic activities and relationships. A number of research projects carried on by rural sociologists are helpful in this regard.

J. H. Kolb and R. A. Polson described more than two decades ago their findings as to the "Changing Role of Service Centers" in Walworth County, Wisconsin.[2] The service centers in and

1. Edgar Z. Palmer, "Some Economic Problems of Clay Center, Nebraska" (Business Research Bulletin No. 54, College of Business Administration, University of Nebraska, 1950), p. 53.
2. J. H. Kolb and R. W. Polson, "Trends in Town-Country Relations" (Research Bulletin 117, Agricultural Experiment Station of the University of Wisconsin and the U.S.D.A. cooperating, September, 1933). See pp. 20-31.

about this county were classified into three major types: (1) "country centers, including the neighborhood or crossroads center and the hamlet or very small village center"; (2) "rurban centers including the village or small town center . . . whose lines of service are only semi-complete, and the larger village or town, and even the small city center, i.e., over 2,500 population, whose services are quite complete"; and (3) "the urban centers including cities of varying types and sizes and the large metropolitan center, Chicago."

According to this study, the earlier self-sufficient community was clearly yielding under pressure of a trend toward specialization, with certain kinds of services or functions tending to move toward certain types of trade centers. The authors pointed out that with the vast improvement in means of communication and travel it was no longer feasible for every trade center to "offer all the services which farm families require." The small "country centers" were becoming important principally "for restricted merchandise (the store around the corner!), for social activities, and for primary educational and religious services." The towns and villages were "increasingly becoming the main centers for many of the services required by country families," gaining "undisputed possession of the major patronage of rural people for major groceries, banking, marketing and high school," serving "a majority with hardware, dry goods, and some forms of recreation, but . . . giving way to the city in ready-to-wear, and in specialized forms of recreation, and of hospital or medical care."

Running through this whole analysis of a rather typical middle-western area, "is the thread of specialization and interdependence. Service centers in the county, whether the primary, crossroads and neighborhood centers, or the larger town-country community centers, were found to be reorganizing and readjusting in order to perform the services for which they are best fitted. In the present competitive situation of freer communication and travel, there is no alternative open to them."

This tendency toward specialization and interdependence was further emphasized in a study by A. H. Anderson and C. J. Miller, published in 1953.[3] These researchers concluded that small business communities now appear to be "in process of adapting themselves to a sort of 'suburban' status, as rural consumers buy certain shopping goods in cities. This adjustment has been by trial and error, and is probably still going on." In Nebraska they found that in general "there are an average of 13 rural satellite towns or villages for each farm city" (2,500 to 25,000 population), and that each rural trade center is confronted with the difficult task of determining which services it can profitably provide in the light of the competitive situation prevailing in the satellite system of which it is a part. They suggest that if a sufficiently large sample of rural towns could be studied, furnishing data as to the types of businesses operating in each class, "a 'model' small-town business community could be projected . . . that . . . could serve as something of a guide to local business ventures."

A broader study of precisely this nature has just been completed for the entire state of Nebraska.[4] With a few minor exceptions, all incorporated places in the state were examined and tabulations made of the various types of business places found in towns of different sizes. Of particular interest here are the findings relative to smaller trade centers which were divided into groups by size, as follows: population 32 to 62; 63 to 124; 125 to 249; 250 to 499; 500 to 999; and 1,000 to 1,999. For each class of town the authors listed the types of business found and indicated the "intensity of appearance" of each. In

3. "The Changing Role of the Small Town in Farm Areas" (Bulletin 419, Bureau of Agricultural Economics, U.S.D.A., and the Experiment Station, University of Nebraska, May, 1953), pp. 21, 28, 31.
4. Leonard Tobkin and Edgar Z. Palmer, "Types of Business in Nebraska Towns" (Business Research Bulletin No. 57, College of Business Administration, University of Nebraska, 1954). See especially pp. 55-6.

towns with population from 125 to 249, for example, practically all had a grocery store and a general auto repair shop; about half had a restaurant, farm equipment dealer, lumber yard, hay-grain-feed store, food locker, blacksmith shop, and barber; and approximately one-fourth had a plumbing and heating firm, petroleum wholesaler, produce assembler, new and used car dealer, appliance store, drug store, liquor store, beauty shop, and bank.

Space does not permit a detailed summary here, but the complete report is available in printed form to anyone who is interested. This research is relevant primarily to the Great Plains region, but it represents a type of research which can be expected eventually to help small towns throughout the entire nation which are trying to determine the types of business which are most appropriate to them. Studies of this nature are admittedly only a guide to businessmen and cannot be applied in any given case without careful examination of special circumstances, but even so, they provide a factual base which is conducive to intelligent action.

Improving Retail Services

For a variety of reasons not easily isolated from each other, the small-town place of business is often a drab, colorless institution. The unpainted, antiquated store front and its dusty show window littered with boxes and other uninteresting objects is dreadfully common. Equally widespread are store arrangements and merchandising practices which are completely out of harmony with modern standards. In the era of the cracker barrel, spittoon, and ring of chairs around a pot-bellied iron stove, such things may have been relatively insignificant. Even if trade were taken to a larger neighboring town, the horse and buggy trip was deucedly inconvenient and the situation there might not have been very different. But today we are living in a different age.

The average modern city, large or small, has its quota of

neat, streamlined and well-stocked stores, with merchants who are fairly conversant with up-to-date business procedures. Access to such city stores has grown easier and more convenient for the farmer and villager as the years have passed. Distance is now a relatively minor factor, and rural residents everywhere are kept constantly informed about goods available in cities through radio, television, and other advertising media. The small-town merchant is truly in competition with the city merchant.

As was pointed out in the foregoing section, the village businessman must decide what services he can successfully offer in view of his satellite relationship to urban competitors in his region. But once this decision has been made, he can by no means relax on the assumption that the people of his rural trade area will automatically come to him for the things he offers for sale. Even groceries, which normally are considered the prerogative of the small-town trade center, will be purchased in considerable measure from urban competitors if the rural merchant is lax. In this day of canned goods and commodious deep freezers, the rural consumer can be quite independent of the home-town grocer who refuses to advance beyond the cracker-barrel pattern. There is, of course, a point beyond which it will not be profitable for small-town storekeepers to invest time and money in the improvement of their business establishments, but for large numbers this point is probably quite remote.

Though more attention must be given to the problem of making the rural business firm an efficient and attractive place in which to trade, it is not the purpose of this chapter to outline principles and procedures which can be applied to attain this goal. Instead, we shall touch upon a few general approaches to the problem which may encourage the development of a sound basis for specific action.

In the first place, the importance of a constructive attitude on the part of local businessmen should be emphasized. Defeatism is common among small-town merchants who are losing business to neighboring city firms, and their attitude is certainly not difficult to understand. "The handwriting is on the wall. Why try to fight the inevitable? What's the use of trying to buck a current that will eventually overwhelm us anyway?"

In some instances there admittedly *is* nothing that can be done. There always have been small towns headed for extinction, and there probably always will be. Present trends, however, do not point toward the disappearance of the rural trading center, but rather toward a readjustment in which it finds its appropriate economic role in relation to the increasingly competitive urban trade centers. It is quite essential, therefore, that the merchants of the small town resist any attitude that their cause is lost, because this normally leads to inactivity, negativism and mental sluggishness. They must be realistic, to be sure, but realism is not synonymous with an admission of defeat. A truly realistic approach calls for a critical and objective examination of the factors involved, followed by sustained effort to make the most of every available opportunity.

There are those who regard as superficial any stress upon the importance of spirit in a community, but such men are hardly conversant with the economic history of their own country. The industrial and agricultural frontiers of the United States were conquered by men and women of courage, vision and enthusiasm, not by those who felt that Indian hazards, sparse rainfall, insect pests, engineering difficulties, and a thousand and one other stumbling blocks would make further progress hopeless. We have no reference here to the occasional outburst of community spirit in certain localities which is followed by a period of stupor. What is crucial is a constructive attitude which inspires the local business element to constant effort toward advancement for itself and for its community. This is intangible, but very real.

In addition, experience indicates that some type of businessmen's organization is highly desirable. Wherever possible, this ought to include farmers as well as merchants and professional people, because all are deeply involved in the business life of the small community.

The structure of the organization will naturally be determined by local needs. In larger villages there is often a regular Chamber of Commerce with a volunteer, part-time, or even a full-time secretary, but this is hardly appropriate for a hamlet-centered community having only a few business places. In these smaller localities, a Community Club with a standing committee on business improvement may serve the purpose. Elsewhere, a Lions Club or a Commercial Club will provide the necessary framework for the job to be done.

Whatever the form of organization may be, every community should have a well-defined unit of some kind which assumes responsibility for the promotion of business activity. Many small towns have existed for years without a group of this kind, but it is safe to assume that most of them have thereby been hampered in the realization of their full business potential. There is undoubtedly much that the individual businessman, acting alone, can do to improve his business, but the fact remains that he will probably do these things better if he enjoys the benefit of regular get-togethers with fellow merchants where new ideas are obtained and old ideas are examined through discussion and study.

Furthermore, it is clear that the number of customers attracted to a given store will be determined not only by action that the owner himself may undertake, but also by factors of community-wide scope over which he personally has very little control. A dusty, muddy main street or lack of adequate parking facilities may easily drive potential customers to neighboring towns, but what can Mr. Hardware Dealer do about it individually if the Town Board drags its feet or has no funds to remedy the situation? Much trade may be lost to a town which lies just off a major highway if there is no attractive sign showing the best way to the business district. The writer knows of one such village of 1,000 population where anyone but the well acquainted must play peek-a-boo down several streets before chancing upon the thoroughfare which takes him to the central square. These and similar problems which affect business adversely can often be solved by local business and professional men working jointly, but where no organ exists through which united action can occur, the problems are usually left hanging in mid-air.

There is another noteworthy advantage in having a commercial organization or committee in the small community. It provides a convenient arrangement for getting together with the businessmen of other localities where similar groups exist. An invaluable cross-fertilization of ideas can occur through state or regional conferences of Chambers of Commerce or through joint meetings or projects of commercial groups from neighboring communities.

Another approach toward better service by the small town businessman lies in consistent reading of trade journals and books related to his field of endeavor. Creative minds the nation over are working ceaselessly to develop new techniques for improving business practices, and most of the really bright ideas eventually appear in print. In every trade or profession, it is the mentally alert person who moves ahead, the person who keeps his eyes and ears open for better ways of doing his job. To close one's eyes to the printed page as a source of enlightenment and inspiration, as many people regrettably do, is to reveal a static frame of mind which is not well adapted to a changing world.

Finally, the rural businessman will find it helpful occasionally to call upon capable outside help in diagnosing his difficulties and in revising strategy. The local man is often so close to his situation that he fails to detect weaknesses which are obvious to an outsider.

Developing Small-Town Industry

Earle Hitch has made the following statement regarding future possibilities of industrial development in rural areas:

"Now is the time for small communities to experiment with change; to act with daring and determination. For Rural America is on the brink of a tumbling transition. Now, for the first time since the factory system put an end to the old handicrafts, industrial expansion is taking a turn that can be made favorable to the rural environments. . . . Manufacturing is no longer confined to the city."[5]

The trend toward greater industrial activity in rural areas is already well under way, with developments occurring on two major fronts. First, there is the "home grown" small industry, and second, the "imported" firm or branch. Each of these will be considered briefly in turn.

Many a small town has gone all out to lure industry from distant climes to its rural haven of economic opportunity, all the while belittling and failing to support some local genius whose only serious fault lay in his home-town citizenship. Not that a budding industrial enterpriser should be coddled by his fellow townsmen! But one would assume that he might at least be entitled to encouragement and assistance commensurate with that accorded an outsider.

The small community needs to look more carefully for potential industrial developments in its own back yard. Ordinarily, the beginnings of a small local industry are inconspicuous, but there are thousands of examples of such firms throughout the nation which have become robust going concerns, contributing substantially to local economic stability and, indirectly, to the cultural enrichment of community life. One such enterprise is Nebraska Plastics, Inc., of Cozad, the story of which has been briefly related as follows:[6]

> Just before World War II, Milo German, a Cozad farmer (and now owner of Nebraska Plastics) was searching for better irriga-

5. Earle Hitch, *Rebuilding Rural America* (New York: Harper & Brothers, 1950), p. 25.
6. *Nebraska on the March* (Lincoln: Division of Nebraska Resources, State Capitol), October, 1954, pp. 6-7.

tion methods to utilize on land he owned in Dawson County. He, along with a good many other land owners in the area, wanted to find a way to take an even flow of water from irrigation ditches into the field rows. Also sought was a controlled flow, with less labor, less water waste and improved quality and crop yields through better irrigation.

None of the methods used at that time—primarily those of cutting the ditch banks with a shovel or running water through the bank by use of buried lathe boxes—were very satisfactory. Cutting the ditch banks produced uneven openings and weakened the ditches, causing them to wash out often. Plugging of the lathe boxes by floating trash meant no water at all for some rows. Any method of running the water through the ditch bank had big drawbacks.

To correct these deficiencies, German conceived the idea of taking the water over the top of the ditch bank by use of a siphon-gravity system utilizing a curved tube whose discharge end was in the field row and whose intake end was below the water surface —below floating trash in the ditch. Early experiments were made with discarded steam coupling hoses used to connect railroad cars and old bicycle tires cut in half. While far from perfect, this system was far superior to the old methods.

The real "break" with the new idea came a short while later when an Omaha plumbing wholesaler displayed some straight lengths of light-weight, transparent, plastic tubing. Four hundred feet of tubing, enough for 100 siphon tubes of four-foot lengths, was purchased and taken to Cozad for experimentation. The problem then was to devise a method of bending these four-foot straight lengths so that they would curve over the bank from the ditch water to the field rows.

. . . From 1941 to 1947, the tubes were manufactured from already made plastic pipe. In 1947, the company bought extruding machinery and has been making its own pipe and siphon tubes since then. . . .

This year a new economy line of "Cozad" tubes was added. The new tube is made of black Polyethylene and with this recent addition the company now offers the most complete line of transparent and non-transparent irrigation siphons in the world. Whereas the

> tubes were at first sold just to local farmers, they are now sold in most of the irrigated areas of the world, including 23 foreign countries.
>
> . . . In combinations of length, diameter, bends and material types, Nebraska Plastics now makes more than 1,500 different kinds of siphon tubes—all serving a specific purpose. The company has an average of 35 employees who, during the busy season, are dispersed on a three-shift, around-the-clock operation.

Recent decades have seen a substantial development of our natural resources through regional conservation projects in the great river valleys of the United States. Under the Missouri River Basin Development Program (the Pick-Sloan Plan and its successors), to name just one example, huge quantities of hydroelectric power will eventually flow from generators installed at strategic points along the Old Muddy. According to government estimates, "the Missouri Basin plan contemplates the installation, all together, of almost 1,500,000 kilowatts of power capacity, with a potential output well above 5½ billion kilowatt-hours annually. Irrigation requirements will absorb 900 million kilowatt-hours a year, leaving over 4½ billion for industrial and commercial purposes."[7] Such additional power resources should be a strong stimulus to industrial development in rural areas.

We live in an age of big industry, but small industry in the small town also has its place. As Arthur E. Morgan has stated in reference to the many thousands of active small industries in the United States: "They are not chiefly surviving vestiges of a passing social order, but to a large degree are normal, integral elements of modern industrial life."[8]

In addition to a further expansion of indigenous industries, as described above, the small community can look forward to

7. *Putting the Missouri to Work* (Washington, D. C.: Bureau of Reclamation, Department of the Interior, 1945), p. 13.
8. Arthur E. Morgan, *Industries for Small Communities* (Yellow Springs, Ohio: Community Service, Inc., 1953), p. 12.

the transplanting of additional firms from urban areas under the industrial decentralization movement which is now gaining momentum. For a variety of reasons, there is a growing tendency for urban industries to seek rural sites for themselves or for their branches. The reasons are primarily economic, relating to taxes, labor supply, raw materials, transportation, markets, and the like, but the threat of atomic warfare is at least a subconscious factor in the situation. Val Peterson, as Civil Defense Administrator, has stated that "it is now certain that any of our large cities could be gutted by the H-bomb. Thus it becomes imperative that more of our industries move into the rural areas, in a realistic and orderly fashion, in order to break up the concentrations of factories which make such attractive H-bomb targets."[9]

Whatever the causes of industrial dispersion may be, there is intense competition among the less populous municipalities for the industries which are seeking new sites. Active in this struggle are many towns and villages in rural areas. The small town, however, has an uphill battle, for it must provide not only the economic resources required by a given industry, but also the many types of cultural opportunities which modern industry desires for its workers.[10] The latter requirement is a serious obstacle for the small town in quest of industry.

Perhaps a solution might be found through some kind of cooperative arrangement among a number of rural communities in the general vicinity of a proposed plant site. If a town of 1,000 population, for example, could not afford to build a swimming pool or other essential recreation facilities, possibly the people of two or three neighboring communities could be induced to help contribute the necessary funds. Local

9. Quoted in Donald S. Stroetzel, "Those New Jobs in American Towns," *Pathfinder . . . Town Journal,* May, 1954, p. 70.

10. For a statement on this point by Don G. Mitchell, president of Sylvania Electric Products, Inc., see H. Clay Tate, *Building a Better Home Town* (New York: Harper & Brothers, 1954), pp. 25-6.

jealousies make this a very difficult approach. As one man put it who was asked to make a contribution for a hospital to be built in a neighboring village: "I'll give anything for the improvement of my own community, but I'll be damned if I'll give a single cent for something in any other town!" Nevertheless, if the people of a given area recognized a sufficient potential gain for themselves in terms of new employment opportunities and additional business volume, they might conceivably be induced to cooperate with neighboring communities in quest of new industry. Intercommunity cooperation toward this end is an uncharted course, but it appears worthy of consideration by the rural community which, alone, lacks sufficient facilities to be attractive as an industrial site.

Not all communities are interested in promoting industrial development. While most urban centers welcome and seek it, there are some which exhibit an outright unfriendly attitude toward industrial newcomers. Among rural communities there is a similar divergence of attitude. Many wish to remain undisturbed as peaceful retail trade centers, while others endeavor to forge ahead to manufacturing. An example of the latter is the Nebraska hamlet of Holstein (population 187) which in 1953 organized Holstein Improvement, Inc., with an authorized capital of $25,000. The corporation was authorized to buy land, construct buildings, and otherwise assist business and industry.[11]

In determining local policy, a given community will weigh the possible disadvantages of new industry against potential benefits. On the one hand, there may be serious readjustment problems in their schools, utilities, housing, recreation facilities, parking, et cetera. On the other, a sound industrial development may lend a much-needed stability to the economy of the community, particularly in agricultural areas. The added payroll dollars may increase business activity, with favorable effects on many aspects of community living. But most important of all, new industry may provide job opportunities for many of the

11. *Nebraska on the March,* February, 1953, p. 2.

fine young people who each year find it necessary to leave the farms and small towns for urban centers in search of a chance to make a living.

Numerous publications are available to communities, large or small, which desire to develop along this line. Among these is a helpful bulletin entitled "The Community Development Survey: The First Step in a Community Industrial Expansion Program," published by the Chamber of Commerce of the United States, and another called "Basic Industrial Location Factors," Industrial Series No. 74, which is available through the U. S. Department of Commerce. In addition, most states have public agencies of some kind from which advice and assistance can be obtained.

8

COMMUNITY RECREATION

A good cause makes a stout heart and a strong arm.—PROVERB

ALL PEOPLE TAKE PART in recreation of some type or other, but often it is looked upon as a diversion from life rather than as an integral part of it—a way of occasionally "getting away from it all." Many a professional person, farmer, homemaker or laborer plans the daily work program carefully but gives attention to recreation only if there happens to be time for it. Indeed, some people have a feeling of guilt when they take time out to play while there is still work to be done (and there is always work to be done).

Reasonable time spent at play does not conflict with work. It tends, on the contrary, to increase output and to improve the quality of work done. Further, the person who engages in a balanced leisure-time program is likely to enjoy more pleasant relationships with his associates than he who is always too busy making a living or saving the world to have a little fun.

W. I. Thomas referred to man as having four basic wishes, all of which are rooted in his biological inheritance and in the cultural environment in which he develops. These wishes are for security, response (love and friendship), recognition (a place in the sun), and new experience. The wish for new experience includes the desire for recreational activity of all kinds and is fundamental not only in the sense that it is world-wide, but also because it applies to all age groups.

Many communities falter in relation to the latter. They recognize the need for play in the life of a youngster but somehow seem to believe that as people grow older, the need for play progressively diminishes until in old age it becomes virtually non-existent. To crystallize this erroneous belief, society has designated a role for the aged which almost eliminates recreational activity, and we therefore find that communities ordinarily pay little or no attention to this important age group in planning their recreational programs.

The urge for recreation is life-long. Remarkable changes admittedly do occur in the type of recreation enjoyed by an individual as he progresses through life; witness the irritation suffered by an elderly gentleman exposed to a teen-age Bebop session. But it is wrong to assume that a person has lost his urge for recreation merely because he no longer manifests a personal interest in the activities which he enjoyed as a youth or which young people today seem to enjoy. Recreational activity should be a bona fide part of all human living. It is not only legitimate, but personally and socially essential. No individual life can be satisfying and stable without it. It follows that no community can be considered good which does not provide adequate recreational facilities and programs for its citizens.

One of the prime requisites of a sound community recreation program is a belief on the part of the general public that it is essential. This is true in urban areas where Mr. John Q. Public ultimately controls the tax funds which are needed to provide the facilities and professional leadership required. In the rural community, however, he not only holds the purse strings but in addition must frequently offer his services as a volunteer in relation to both the planning and implementation of the program. Professional recreational leadership is relatively scarce in the small community setting, and volunteer workers must do a large share of the work if it is to be done at all. This means that people must see the importance of having a program, not only to the extent of helping to pay for it, but also of making their services available as volunteers, if needed.

Most small communities are not sufficiently aware of the need for a well-rounded community program to do much about it. There is a widespread tendency to limit the program to a series of planned activities for the teen-age group, and even here it often does not gain momentum until an act of juvenile delinquency shocks the general public to action. Sociologists have long recognized a relationship between the lack of wholesome recreational opportunities and juvenile delinquency, but it should be stressed that recreation is not something which must be justified as a solution to certain social ills. It is entitled to a place in its own right, and it is only where this is fully recognized that an acceptable program can be developed and maintained.

One of the important things to which a community should give attention when it desires to develop a recreational program is organization. What sort of structure will best enable us to get the job done? Should we have a central committee of some kind or a decentralized program under which the American Legion, the various churches and other interested groups conduct special programs in which they happen to have a particular interest?

Experience indicates that even in the smallest communities some type of central planning or coordinating group is helpful. This is not to imply that good programs can exist only in communities where a unified planning approach is employed. It does mean, however, that any given community will probably achieve best results if the various groups and individuals interested in doing something to promote wholesome recreation get their heads together in planning, if not in conducting, their program. Some of the more obvious advantages of a unified approach might be stated as follows:

First, it represents a cooperative effort toward the solution of a common problem, and this tends to strengthen the ability of people to work together. Second, a unified approach to community recreation tends to foster the development of a complete program. As long as several groups are operating independently of each other there is a possibility that each will not be fully aware of what the others are doing. This often leaves serious gaps or may lead to duplication of effort with consequent wasteful competition. Where joint planning exists, it is not difficult to check for major deficiencies in the over-all program, and the likelihood of overlapping activities will be diminished. In addition, the chances of continuity from year to year are greater than where complete decentralization prevails.

Third, resources are more easily identified where cooperative planning occurs. In one rural community a dilapidated old pool hall was converted into an attractive youth center. In another, an aged building on Main Street which had successively housed almost every business in town was through volunteer labor and donations converted into a delightful community hall. It is safe to assume that the chances of bringing such resources to light and developing them are at a maximum where a free exchange of ideas exists among the various elements of the community which have an interest in recreation.

Finally, the problem of financing a community recreation program is often simplified through joint effort. In union there is strength, financially as in other ways, and a unified approach tends to convince the Doubting Thomases in a community that the cause is worthy of their support.

As to the type of organization which should be established to develop a community recreation program, there is no single answer. In general, it should be reasonably representative of the entire community and geared to the particular needs of the local situation. Among the common arrangements in small communities are the following:

Volunteer Committee. The recreational program of the hamlet-centered community is often spearheaded by a small group of interested citizens who see that there is a job to be done and go ahead and do it. No one appoints them, and they are responsible to no one. They serve without pay, receiving only the praise or blame which the community chooses to bestow upon them for their efforts.

A few examples will serve to clarify this type of arrangement. In one small community there were five people who were disturbed at the lack of recreational activities for their children and youth and who began to meet informally to discuss the situation. As an outgrowth of these get-togethers they organized themselves as a Recreation Committee and appointed one of their members to serve as chairman. The body was self-perpetuating, and for five years, at this writing, it has planned and conducted a modest but effective summer program. In another community a similar lack of anything "for our young people to do" impelled a middle-aged married couple to rent the town hall and sponsor weekly square dances for all local teen-agers who were interested in coming. In a third locality a local pastor became convinced that the time for action had come when a screaming cat was thrown through an open window into a room where a church choir was in rehearsal. He promptly gathered a number of interested adults and young people about him, and through their efforts a run-down old building was converted into a youth center which provided wholesome recreation three evenings weekly for teen-agers from the entire surrounding area.

The disadvantages of such volunteer committee arrangements are not hard to detect. The programs established tend to be intermittent and of short duration because they are so completely dependent upon the continued interest of a few individuals, who may leave the community, become disillusioned, or just feel that they "can't take it any longer." The fact that there is no permanently established body to which the committee is responsible and from which it derives support is also significant. On the other hand, it is certainly through just such volunteer groups that thousands of small communities are able to conduct community-wide programs which in many instances would otherwise not exist at all.

Club Sponsorship. In other localities, responsibility for planning and implementing a community recreation program is placed in the hands of a committee appointed for that purpose by an already existing civic-interest organization such as a Chamber of Commerce, Community Club, or Community Council. As an illustration of how this operates, let us look briefly at a certain Community Club. Among the standing committees of the Club was one on recreation. The committee members were selected on the basis of special interest or ability along this line and had responsibility for studying the recreational needs and resources of the community and developing plans for a well-balanced program on behalf of the Community Club. The program was financed from Club funds and through voluntary contributions from other sources. It was a privately sponsored program except, of course, for the fact that the park and playground facilities used were public property.

Public Sponsorship. The larger a community, the greater the likelihood that recreation will be regarded as a public function, both as to facilities and program. In urban areas the public nature of this activity is generally taken for granted, and tax funds are used to pay for it. This is true also in many of the larger rural communities, but as one descends the population scale there is an increasing tendency toward financing both the program and facilities independently of tax resources. The practical difficulties of a tax-supported program in a small town include meager assessed valuations and legal limitations on mill levies for recreational purposes. Where the proceeds of the maximum mill levy are insufficient to finance an adequate program, it becomes necessary to tap voluntary sources in addition.

An illustration of a publicly sponsored program supported by taxation and supplemented from other sources is that in

Seward, Nebraska (2,500 population), where a Recreation Board is appointed by the mayor. The structure and functions of this body are indicated in their constitution:

Article I

Name

The name of this organization shall be Seward Recreation Board.

Article II

Purpose

The purpose of this organization shall be:

a. To study the recreational needs of the Seward Community.
b. To develop ways and means of meeting the recreational needs of all age groups within the community.
c. To serve as a clearing house for the coordination of the various recreational programs and activities within the community.
d. To make recommendations to the City Council and to interested organizations as to facilities, activities and personnel which would help to provide a well-rounded program of community recreation.
e. To submit annually to the City Council a statement of proposed income and expenditures for the implementation of plans developed by the Recreation Board.
f. To supervise the soliciting of funds needed to carry out the recreational plans approved by the City Council.

Article III

Membership

The membership shall consist of a representative from:

a. The City Council, Park Board, School Board, City Planning Board, Superintendent of City Schools.
b. Such others as shall be designated by the City Council.

The members under paragraph b, above, shall be appointed for a two-year term and shall be limited to two successive terms.

Article IV

Officers

The officers shall be President, Vice President, Secretary and Treasurer.

Officers shall be elected by majority vote at the annual meeting for one-year terms and shall be nominated by informal ballot. The two highest nominees for each office shall be voted on by informal ballot.

Article V

Quorum

A quorum shall consist of 60 per cent of the total membership.

Article VI

Meetings

The regular meeting shall be held on the third Monday of each month at 8:00 P.M., with special meetings subject to call by the president.

The regular February meeting shall be the annual meeting.

Article VII

Amendments

Amendments to this constitution may be presented at any regular meeting and voted on at any subsequent meeting. A two-thirds vote of the members present shall be required to pass an amendment.

Article VIII

This constitution shall go into effect upon approval by the City Council.

One of the most common reasons given for the lack of an adequate recreation program in the small community is: "We just don't have the leaders!" Anyone who has lived in a small community knows that this explanation is not without foundation. Where a problem of this kind exists, however, it is ordinarily not a clear-cut either-or proposition. The fact that there is no one at the moment who can step in and call square dances, for example, is no proof that potential leadership does not exist which could be made functional with a little training or experience. To elaborate our treatment of this subject in Chapter 6, let us offer here a few specific suggestions for the small community which experiences difficulty in finding recreation leaders.

Plans for a needed program should not be dropped simply because adequate leadership is not readily available. The difference between a progressive community in which things happen and one which just can't get going often lies in the community's attitude at this very point. A common tendency is to just drop the whole idea, at least for the present, hoping that some day someone will come along who can do the job. A more realistic and constructive approach is to accept the lack of leaders as only a surface phenomenon and then proceed to find a solution.

A helpful first step is to take an inventory of recreational leadership resources in the community, giving special attention to personal backgrounds, interests, and attitudes related to the field of recreation. The names of all persons who might be able to make a contribution should be listed, and the nature of the talent possessed indicated after each name. The list obtained will probably include a considerable number of items such as the following:

Mrs. Grace Smith, former Den Mother in Cub Scout program—handicraft
Rev. Frank Anderson—tennis
John Jones—has done considerable square dancing and might become a "caller."
Mrs. Henry Jacks, former elementary school teacher—story-telling and games for younger children
Howard Mitchell—baseball

An inventory of this kind helps to uncover talent which might not come to light if a less painstaking search were made, and it reveals a nucleus around which the program may be built, particularly if only local volunteer leaders can be used, as is often the case in a small community.

Second, a watch should be kept for leadership-training institutes and short courses to which potential leaders can be sent. Such courses are presented regularly throughout the nation by many voluntary groups, exemplified in the Middle West by the Iduhapi Recreation Leaders Laboratory of Minneapolis, Danebod Folk School at Tyler, Minnesota, and the Great Plains Recreation Leaders Training Institute. Opportunities for training are also frequently provided by the state's agricultural extension service and by other public agencies.

It is surprising how much a person attending one of these institutes can learn in a short time, not only about the recreational activity of his choice but also about the art of teaching it to others. In addition, he often gains the confidence necessary to assume a leadership role when he returns to his home community. A small community shows good judgment when it encourages its leaders or potential leaders to take advantage of available training opportunities. In fact, it is a good investment to help such persons meet the rather modest cost of attending.

A further approach in the search for leadership talent is to examine neighboring communities. If the desired talent is not available at home, perhaps it may be found elsewhere. A leader from another community may not be too favorably inclined toward working in your program, but a slight remuneration for his trouble will go a long way toward overcoming this reluctance.

Let us turn now to the recreation program itself. It is an axiom of community improvement that no sure-fire, ready-made pattern exists which can be followed in all localities. This applies to recreation as well as to other phases of community life. If suitable blueprints were available for recreation programs in communities of different sizes, the situation in our small communities would probably be far better than it is today. But blueprints must conform to needs, and the needs of each community are peculiar to itself.

The program in any given community must be developed in the light of factors such as the following: interests and desires of the people, partial programs already existing in the community and in neighboring localities, leadership resources and physical facilities available, financial resources which can be tapped, age and sex composition of the population, number and distribution of people to be served. It is quite essential that the local situation be studied before determining the content of the program.

A mistake sometimes made by the committee-in-charge is to assume that it knows what the people want without asking them. In one community a group of well-intentioned adults decided that their teen-agers needed a youth center and proceeded with plans for its development. For some reason the young people had not been involved in the planning operations, and it was not until the adults were ready to sign the lease for the quarters to be used that they by chance discovered the real attitude of the youngsters toward the project. The latter were quite uninterested and uncooperative because they saw no need whatever for a youth center and, in fact, felt that the whole project was being imposed from above.

All too often the adults of rural communities establish recreational programs for youth without even bothering to consult them as to their interests, to say nothing of inviting them to participate in the planning process. This is probably due less to malicious intent on the part of the adults than to a feeling that the young people do not know what is good for them or that they are too immature to make a significant contribution. However, the experience of communities which have brought young people into the planning process bears eloquent witness to the fact that the judgment and acumen of youth are grossly underrated by most adults.

It is likewise presumptuous to plan leisure-time programs for any other age-groups without affording them ample opportunity to express their ideas as to what should be included and how they should be administered. It is only through careful consultation with, or better yet, through active participation of, the group to be served that a satisfactory program can be developed.

A good community recreation program must be built upon factual information pertinent to the local situation. How these facts can best be gathered will have to be determined by the community itself. In some instances there are ready-made self-analysis forms which can be used to good advantage. Among these are: "Cultural Arts and Recreation, Outline for Identifying Problems and Resources," Tomorrow's Community Worksheet No. 2 (CDG-4), Agricultural Extension Service, Iowa State College, Ames, Iowa; "Community Evaluation Sheet for Recreation" (12-page mimeographed bulletin), Community Service Bureau, Extension Division, University of Virginia, Charlottesville, Virginia; "For the Recreation Committee," pages 288-98 in *Democracy Is You—A Guide to Citizen Action,* by Richard W. Poston.

In other instances, a community will do better by starting from scratch and developing its own survey forms. This was done in Bennet, a small village-centered community in eastern Nebraska. For several years a summer recreation program had been conducted, consisting of a Saturday night supervised play period for children, followed by free open-air movies for everyone. The committee in charge was uncertain as to community sentiment toward the program. How did the parents feel about it? The youngsters? Did the farmers want the program again? How could it be improved? Should paid leadership be employed?

To obtain answers to such questions, two brief questionnaires were devised and circulated, one among parents and the other among pupils in the public school. The response revealed, first, a strong sentiment among parents and children in favor of continuing the Saturday night programs and, second, a definite feeling that local volunteer talent rather than outside hired help should be used in supervising the children's play period. Further, the committee was given a clear vote of confidence based upon past performance and could therefore proceed with assurance.

Check lists and questionnaires such as those referred to above can be used to discover the interests and desires of a community along recreational lines and to ascertain public evaluation of existing programs. Information of both types is essential to successful programming.

A simple but very helpful set of guideposts for building a recreation program can be obtained in mimeographed form from the National Recreation Association, 315 Fourth Avenue, New York City. It bears the title "What Is Included in a Local Year-Round Recreation Program" (M.B. #105-5-31) and offers numerous suggestions as to principles which must be kept in mind, as well as an extensive list of activities which can be included. Among the principles stressed are the following:

Community Recreation
...provides for all age groups
...is a problem for all communities, regardless of size
...provides for a broad program of activities
...strives for a number of definite objectives
...strives to meet the need for recreation in all the different periods of free time
...uses existing facilities and secures additional needed facilities
...is carried on with the active help and cooperation of many organized groups

Another valuable resource for program planners is a bulletin entitled "Planning Recreation for Rural Home and Community," available for 30 cents from the Superintendent of Documents, Government Printing Office, Washington 25, D.C. It is a publication of the U. S. Department of Agriculture, Extension Service (AIB 20), issued in 1950.

9

THE COMMUNITY SCHOOL

Upon the education of the people of this country the fate of this country depends.—BENJAMIN DISRAELI

THE RURAL COMMUNITY is confronted with many problems in public education. Modern transportation, improved roads and a declining farm population are making obsolete the traditional arrangement under which small country schools dotted the landscape, but the tasks of redistricting and consolidation are complicated and fraught with emotion. The level of professional training required of elementary school teachers in some rural states is disturbingly low, but there is slight prospect of raising certification requirements without also raising the salary scales. Adequate financial support for well-rounded educational programs is hampered by antiquated systems of taxation and a lack of economic resources which are characteristic of extensive agricultural regions throughout the nation.

A somewhat less obvious, but equally important, problem is that of building an educational program which is integrated with community living. Too often the educational process relates only to textbooks and other source materials found within the four walls of the schoolhouse and disregards the wealth of teaching materials existing in the community around it. Too often, again, the educational program directly affects only the children of compulsory school age, hardly recognizing the urgent need of the adult population for lifelong learning in a complex and rapidly changing world. It is with these two facets of rural education that the present chapter will deal.

Effective Use of Community Resources

Some years ago a civics teacher in a small city walked into the City Hall to purchase a tag for her newly acquired poodle. She appeared somewhat bewildered upon entering the building, and revealed in seeking directions that this was her first visit to the City Hall during the twenty years she had taught (civics!) in this community. For two decades she had worked with local youngsters to help them gain an understanding of governmental affairs, and in the process she had totally ignored the one living resource within easy reach which could have been used to show her pupils what their textbooks were talking about.

This is perhaps an extreme example, but it is symbolic of a widespread failure of teachers to utilize local environments as an aid in the instructional process. In fields like vocational agriculture and home economics, there is of course a very intimate relationship between the textbook-classroom situation and the home environment of the student. The effectiveness of this approach is not open to question. In the natural sciences the textbook materials are likewise readily geared to reality through laboratory experiments involving frogs, gases, and chemicals. But in most other subject fields the contacts with surrounding environment have been insufficient.

What, then, are some of the resources that can be tapped to make a rural educational institution more truly a "community school"? How can the rural community be used as a laboratory to improve the instructional process?

Use of Individuals. Every school has its staff of regular teachers whose assigned task it is to educate the youngsters enrolled. The good teachers do not rely exclusively upon their own abilities in doing this educational job but draw upon the services of others in the community who may have something to contribute. There exists, in effect, a central core of paid teachers surrounded by a wide fringe of potential volunteers who can be used to help educate the child. Often the volunteer teachers are far better informed in certain subject areas than the paid teacher herself, and ordinarily they are glad to lend a hand when called upon. Relevant to the rural curriculum are the activities and backgrounds of the local banker, the merchant, the homemaker, the farmer, the lawyer, the mayor, the police officer, the G.I. who has been stationed in Japan, and the person who has visited the United Nations. For a teacher to overlook or otherwise fail to utilize such personal resources is to deprive her pupils of a broadening and stimulating experience to which they are entitled.

The University of Wyoming has developed an interesting device whereby the teachers in any given school can obtain quick access to information on leadership talent available in the community. It is reproduced in full below:[1]

Dear Parents:

The Newcastle Elementary Schools are interested in building better bridges of understanding between the home and school. We are also anxious to improve our program of education in every possible way. Our plan is based upon the fact that there exist a great many of rich human experience in our community and that children in school should profit from this experience.

Pupils need to realize that people, as well as books, are important sources of information and inspiration, that one person's experience is never completely matched or duplicated by that of any other person. Will you help us provide this more desirable, broader and richer experience for the boys and girls? We need your help in making available more vivid and lifelike learning situations in the classroom.

1. Through the courtesy of Dr. Otto W. Snarr, Supervisor, Extension Classes, Adult Education and Community Service, University of Wyoming.

If you are willing to help, please answer the following questions and return the blank as early as possible.

1. Do you have any of the following hobbies? (please check)

Collecting stamps	—	Making hooked rugs or weaving	—
Collecting old coins	—	Training animals	—
Collecting old books or magazines, or 1st editions	—	Photography	—
Collecting Indian relics	—	Woodworking	—
Tying flies (fishing)	—	Collecting china, glassware or pottery	—

Other (please explain)__________________________

2. Do you have any special experience or talent in:

Art	—	Local or state history	—
Music	—	Traffic safety	—
Sports	—	Transportation	—
Writing	—	Communication	—

3. Do you hold (or have you ever held) an official office in the state or local government? YES__ NO__
   If "yes" give name of position______________________

4. Have you taken any interesting or unusual trips?
   Foreign countries (please list)____________________
   Interesting points in the United States (please list) __________
   ____

5. Check the types of activities you would be willing to engage in at school:
   Will make a short talk __
   Will lead an informal discussion __
   Will give a demonstration __
   Will show filmstrips, slides or movies __
   Will help in conducting a field trip __

6. Do you know of other persons in the community who have had unusual experiences, who hold unusual and interesting positions, who have highly specialized abilities of one type or another. Please list and indicate how they might help.________________
   ____

7. When would it be more convenient for you to help?
   Afternoon —
   Morning —
8. Would you prefer to come to school —; or, have the class visit your home —?
9. Signed____________________
   Address____________________
   Telephone __________ __________
   Business Home

Contact with Local Organizations. An alert teacher will find many possibilities for mutually beneficial relationships between her pupils and the various organizations in the community. Instances are legion where local groups have contributed gladly toward the purchase of band uniforms, musical instruments, recreational equipment, library books, scientific equipment, motion picture projectors, and the like.

Similarly, they have often sponsored the trips of students to festivals and contests of various kinds where school funds have been insufficient. In one rural school district the board of education had a strong negative attitude toward the proposal that they establish a hot-lunch program for the children. They did, however, tell the local Women's Club that "if you are so interested in this project, why don't you go ahead and do it yourselves?" . . . Which is exactly what the ladies did! They gathered money, stoves, utensils and other essential items and finally got the program under way, a program which incidentally became a real drawing-card for pupils who otherwise might not have thought of attending this school.

Community organizations which contribute in this manner to the welfare of the school usually welcome a little service from the students in return. This service can be given in the form of musical numbers at the Chamber of Commerce, a declamation for the Home Extension Club, and posters for the community-wide home talent show. Such courtesies not only help to maintain a friendly and mutually beneficial relationship between the school and community groups but also provide the student body with a highly desirable type of practical educational experience.

Utilization of Community Activities. The day-to-day activities of community living provide many fine educational opportunities for school children. Visits to the local print shop, fire department, creamery, railroad station, doctor's office and other points of interest are helpful in giving the pupil a realistic picture of the topics studied in the classroom.

In our day of rapid transportation, the resources of neighboring communities can also be employed. A trip to the county seat and the office of the Agricultural Extension Service, for instance, is worth while for farm and town children alike. Most of the youngsters in a rural community have seen their County Agent and Home Extension Agent in action, but few have had an opportunity to see the entire program in proper perspective.

The early mistrust of the Agricultural Extension program by farmers throughout the country has largely been replaced by a feeling of confidence, inspired by capable and level-headed work on the part of the county agents. Within any given county, however, there are still families which the Extension program has been unable to reach. Often these are the low-income farm families. It is no easy matter to open the eyes of these unresponsive families to the benefits which could be theirs, but one effective approach to them is through their children. If the youngsters can gain a better understanding of the program through personal contact with Extension personnel, a desire to cooperate may be generated which will gradually infiltrate the home. Any contacts which the school establishes with the Extension program, whether through visits to the county office, field trips to experimental plots, or joint ventures with 4-H Clubs, will thus serve a dual educational purpose: first, it will give the pupils a real understanding of an important subject in their curriculum; and second, it will tend to promote greater utilization of Agricultural Extension resources by rural families.

The Physical Environment as a Resource. Mother Nature is a great ally of the teacher who understands and appreciates her. She provides an endless stream of life and life-processes which can be used to enliven and enrich the educational program. Where, even in modern textbooks, does one find pictures or descriptions of trees, flowers, snowflakes, rocks, birds and clouds which compare in immediacy with the natural phenomena encountered as one steps outside the rural schoolhouse?

Each geographical area has its own natural resources, which are available to the teacher as instructional aids. It is essential that the teacher identify these resources and lay careful plans for utilizing them as fully as possible. Where this is not done, the whole procedure is apt to become a hit-and-miss affair of little value to the child. The rural school has a distinct advantage over its urban counterpart when it comes to nature study, because the source materials are so close at hand. Nature alone, however, does an inadequate job of teaching. The mind of the average human being simply is not conditioned to absorb the wonders of the world about him. Where a good teacher and Mother Nature work together, however, the results can be remarkable.

Adaptation of Curriculum to Ethnic Background. The United States today occupies a position of world leadership which entails many new contacts with the nations of the world. Under the Point-Four program, the Technical Assistance program of the United Nations, the various exchange programs, and a great many other working arrangements, Americans are serving abroad as never before. The effectiveness of such service has often been diminished, however, by our representatives' unfamiliarity with the languages concerned. Interpreters can be used, to be sure, but are hardly conducive to the development of the close personal relationship so often essential.

The fact is that the United States has entered upon a phase of its history where more and more citizens are needed who are capable of speaking two or more languages. In spite of this very obvious trend, there are schools by the hundreds which are failing to utilize local cultural resources toward this end. There is something wrong in a midwestern Czech community, for example, which offers only Latin or French as a foreign language. A tremendous cultural resource exists in the Czech heritage of such a community, and capable bilinguists could be developed for generations to come with minimum effort if the school would only take advantage of the culture base which exists and include the Czech language in its program. Where local ethnic background is disregarded by the school, as it usually is, a genuine community resource is lost by default.

Askov is a small Danish community in Minnesota which for years had a program in which the songs, folklore, history, and literature of Denmark were taught on a voluntary basis in the public school. In the elementary grades the children were offered from 20 to 30 minutes of Danish daily, taught by a special instructor; and a regular two-year course in Danish language, literature and composition was included in the high school curriculum. This program helped to develop linguistic skills which are becoming increasingly important for our country today. In addition, it served to identify the public school closely with the culture of the community of which it was a part.

Adult Education

As described in the foregoing section, the community school draws as fully as possible upon local community resources in carrying on its educational endeavors.

A second important characteristic is that it provides a program which meets the needs of the entire community, not confining its efforts solely to the children of compulsory school age. A splendid foreign example of a rural school serving both children and adults is found in Impington Village, near the University of Cambridge, which was visited by the writer during the winter of 1947. The headmaster of this unique English institution, referring to education as a "continuous" process, said that he and his staff evaluated their work with the children of compulsory school age largely in terms of whether or not they returned, after graduation, to participate in the voluntary adult activities offered.

In the United States there are many urban public schools which have strong educational programs for adults. Formal and informal courses are common along a wide variety of lines, such as child psychology, immigrant English, bookkeeping, cake decorating, driver training, salesmanship, ceramics, American history, and music appreciation—to mention only a few.

But public school adult-education programs are by no means limited to our cities. Marengo, Iowa, for example, has shown conclusively that an effective community-wide program can also be conducted in a rural setting. For nearly two decades this farming community has carried on a program through its public school which has brought town and country together in a remarkable adult-education venture. The program is administered by a seven-member Executive Council of Adult Education which includes the Superintendent of Schools. Working with the Executive Council is an Advisory Council of forty members, consisting of ten persons from each of the following categories: rural women, rural men, town women and town men. Each autumn for ten weeks there are weekly evening classes in approximately fifteen different subjects, determined in advance through a study of community interests and available leadership. The 1952 program, a typical one, offered the following courses to all interested persons, regardless of academic background:

Agriculture
Beginning Sewing
Book Review Course
Figurine Painting
Film Course
Typing
Driver Training
Animal Nutrition and Husbandry
Knitting
Shorthand Refresher Course
Family Relationships
Leather Craft and Leather Tooling
First Aid
Sketching for Fun
Health Course
Public Speaking

The registration fee is $2.00 per course and all classes are held from 8:00 to 9:30 P.M. except on occasions when special events (forum speakers, panel discussions, debates, one-act plays, etc.) are presented. In such instances the regular class work is restricted to one hour, with all participants convening for the special event at 9:00 P.M.

Leadership is on a voluntary basis, drawn largely from the Marengo community itself, but full use is also made of resources such as the Agricultural Extension Service, the University of Iowa, and other nearby educational institutions. A nursery is provided for the convenience of parents who wish to bring children and have them cared for while they attend the sessions of the school.

An attractive booklet describing the "Adult Education Program" is printed each year. According to the Marengo Superintendent of Schools, G. G. Bellamy, the adult-education program is "distinctly a community project," and nothing is left undone to show the local citizens that the success of their program depends upon the extent to which "the people of the community make use of it and contribute to it of their time and talents."

A significant forward step in the area of public school adult-education was taken in 1952, when the National Association of Public School Adult Educators was organized as an affiliate of the Adult Education Association of the U.S.A. Its membership includes educators from urban and rural communities all over the nation where public schools are interested in adult-education programs. The purposes of N.A.P.S.A.E. are outlined in their constitution:

a. To provide a framework for giving leadership to the movement of Adult Education in the public schools.
b. To organize regional and national meetings for the purpose of discussing mutual problems.
c. To provide for the interchange of ideas, including financing and promotion of Adult Education.

d. To provide criteria for the organization of purposeful programs for adults.
e. To study criteria for the analysis of educational needs, project a program of education to meet those needs, and establish a method of evaluation of results.
f. To foster a spirit of cooperation among its members and to awaken in them a keener realization of the opportunities of Adult Education.
g. To promote action programs that may seem best for the professional interests of Adult Education.
h. To define and develop adult education objectives and teaching techniques.

One of the secrets of success in a rural adult-education program lies in maintaining contact with vital sources of inspiration and information concerning the field of public school adult education as a whole. Communication with fellow-educators throughout the nation brings new ideas, suggestions for the solution of knotty problems, help in evaluating one's local efforts, and, perhaps most important of all, the feeling that one is part of a great movement dedicated to building an even greater America through educational programs for adults. Today N.A.P.S.A.E. provides such communication at a modest annual membership fee of $1.00—an opportunity which should not be overlooked by any administrator or teacher who has an interest in this field of action.

Many valuable aids for the local program are also available from the parent organization of N.A.P.S.A.E., the Adult Education Association of the U.S.A. This nation-wide group was formed in the spring of 1951, uniting into a single new organization the American Association for Adult Education and the Department of Adult Education of the National Education Association, both of which had been actively at work for many years. Through its central office at 743 North Wabash Avenue in Chicago, the A.E.A. provides a growing program of services to adult educators and publishes two regular periodicals, *Adult*

Leadership (to which reference has already been made on page 67) and *Adult Education,* a quarterly publication designed primarily for professional workers in the field.

Some years ago the Fund for Adult Education (established by the Ford Foundation) developed a series of nine film-discussion programs under the general title "Great Men and Great Issues in our American Heritage." The purpose of this series is to "provide mature men and women with an opportunity to help themselves gain a better understanding of the problems faced by our country today." Discussion groups are organized locally wherever a dozen or more individuals are interested in attending the nine consecutive sessions and in doing a little reading prior to each session. A typical meeting opens with the showing of a film on a great man, such as Jefferson, and a discussion follows, based upon the film and upon a specially prepared, printed essay on Jefferson which has been circulated in advance and read by all members. Discussion leaders are drawn in rotation from the group itself, and people from all walks of life participate. This first series was followed by others, now available from the Film Council of America, 600 Davis Street, Evanston, Illinois.

Among other worthwhile programs using this approach is that of the American Film Forum, which each month releases a new film wherein some topic of importance in domestic or foreign affairs is discussed by leading authorities. The films serve as springboards for further consideration of the subjects by local discussion groups. Information is available from American Film Forum, Inc., 516 Fifth Avenue, New York 36, New York.

The Great Books Foundation, 37 South Wabash Avenue, Chicago, is another body which provides a carefully devised and popular program for discussion groups. Here the emphasis is upon the reading of books or selections from authors like Plato, Aristotle, Machiavelli, Shakespeare, and Voltaire and upon subsequent discussion of the works read. The 1953 Annual Report of the Foundation stated that its purpose was "to promote adult liberal education through reading and group discussion of selected writings of the most stimulating and influential minds of our civilization."

Hitherto, the Great Books discussion groups have been centered mostly in cities, but the program is certainly as well adapted to the rural community as to the urban. The size of a community has no particular bearing on the success or failure of programs such as those described above. They work well in any community where there is an interest, and it cannot be emphasized too strongly that the public school is a logical spearhead.

One of the problems frequently encountered by the small school in its efforts toward adult education is the lack of suitable physical facilities. Mature men and women are expected to distort their bodies into conformity with seats designed for teenagers, and a rigid seating arrangement makes the desirable informal atmosphere very difficult to attain. This is hardly surprising since most of our school plants were originally planned with little thought of their use for adult programs.

Of special interest in this connection is a current A.E.A. survey of school architecture throughout the United States, with particular reference to facilities for adult education. This study should stimulate school boards and architects to make provision for adult programs in the preparation of building plans for the future.

Before much headway along this line can be made, however, school boards will have to recognize more clearly that they have a responsibility in the field of adult education. Many of them do not see this at all today, and some even go so far as to bar other community agencies from using the schoolhouse for such purposes. But it is a reasonable assumption that the public school of tomorrow will consider more fully in its educational program and architectural design the needs of *all* people in the community. To think otherwise is to undermine the very foundation upon which our growing democracy rests: an enlightened and alert citizenry.

Turning, in conclusion, from the public school, let us examine briefly an institution which long has functioned as a true *community* school. For more than a generation the John C. Campbell Folk School has served as an influential center for the enrichment of rural life and the building of an enlightened citizenship in the mountain areas of southwestern North Carolina. Its philosophical basis is that of the Danish Folk School, but the founders wisely made no effort to transplant the Danish *structure* to North Carolina. Instead, they studied the social and economic needs of the Brasstown region, where the school was to be located, and adapted their institution and its program accordingly. Since farming in the area was inefficient, a school farm was developed, serving as a demonstration center for the best types and methods of farming as recommended by Agricultural Extension workers. They speak today of their modern 366-acre farm with its dairy, poultry and pigs, and 150 acres of woodland as "our laboratory—a farm-laboratory which provides a splendid opportunity to teach simple forest and woodlot practices, improved methods of soil building, and production of family food."

In the Winter School (December through March), which they portray as the heart of their program, the students "learn about American history and culture, farming, living creatively, mountain songs and ballads and folk dancing. They learn to carve ducks, geese, cows, pigs, chickens, horses, dogs and other creatures out of the native woods. They learn to dye wool and weave beautiful rugs and runners. They learn to farm, cook and keep house, and to use modern appliances. They learn, through critical discussions, the meaning of the American way of life, and come to possess a personally satisfying philosophy of living. . . . Emphasis is placed on the heritage of the people and continued development of the sturdy character and fine natural ability of the pioneers. Hence, folk dancing and folk singing are common and much is made of mountain handicrafts. Work, play and song are interspersed with discussions on the historical background of the people and their rightful and necessary place in the wider needs of their country, state, nation and the world. This, plus living together as a family where everyone contributes to the welfare of all, makes learning natural and easy. . . . On Friday nights the people of the community come for moving pictures, now and then a lecture, and always folk singing and folk dancing. They vary in number from sixty to . . . two hundred. Their ages range from three-year-olds to great-grandparents. The spiritual effect is as vital as the evenings are delightful. Back home, work and chores seem lighter."[2] Guided by the motto "I Sing Behind the Plow," the John C. Campbell Folk School has grown out of the soil of its mountain region and, in turn, has had a tremendous impact upon rural living in the entire area.

The quality of social living in a rural community is closely related to the educational and cultural development of its citizens. To this end the *community* school, as interpreted in this chapter, can make a genuine contribution.

2. Frederick L. Brownlee, "The John C. Campbell Folk School" (Brasstown, North Carolina, privately printed).

10

THE CHURCH

To the man who himself strives earnestly, God lends a helping hand.
—AESCHYLUS

THE CHURCH HAS ALWAYS BEEN an important social institution on the American rural scene. Since the earliest days of our history it has been a center not only for religious worship but for a whole network of related social activities as well. By its very nature it affects in some degree, directly or indirectly, every phase of human life.

The basic social significance of the church lies in the influence which it exerts upon the innermost feelings and attitudes of the individual, upon his standards of value, his moral code, and upon the ideals and goals to which his life is dedicated. It is an institution which touches upon the mainsprings of human behavor and is therefore a force to be reckoned with in every phase of individual and community living.

To remain effective in its work as the generations have passed, the church has found it necessary to adapt its structure and program to the changing social conditions. A horse-and-buggy approach to the religious problems of the modern age will not work, and the church which uses it is liable to fall by the way-side with an institutional disease known as "ossification."

By way of illustration, reference might be made to a small rural congregation which had before it the task of selecting a new minister. One faction held that care should be exercised to hire a pastor who liked young people, who knew how to work with them, and who would make a real effort to develop a youth program within the church. The attitude of the majority, however, was expressed by a woman who remarked pointedly: "Oh, why should we worry about a special program for the young people! When we were young [about the turn of the century] we went to church with our parents as a matter of course, and I don't see why our kids can't do the same!"

This woman failed to recognize that the teen-ager of today is far more independent in thought and action than the teen-ager of a generation or two ago and that dozens of interesting and attractive activities beckon to him now which were not competitors with church programs at that time. It is not a foregone conclusion that modern youth will choose to attend a Thursday evening prayer meeting if he has money, transportation, and friends who like to roller skate, dance, bowl, joy ride, go to the movies, swim, play soft ball, or watch wrestlers maul each other on television. Since the church has a different problem now than it had in an earlier day, a new approach is in order.

There are many indications that churches throughout the land are aware of the changing social scene which today calls upon them for adaptation. Increasing emphasis is being placed upon the relationship of the church to the world about it; church programs are including activities of many kinds which were hardly dreamed of fifty years ago; daring experiments in functional church architecture are seen; new ideas in organization and administration are being tried; and interdenominational cooperative efforts are being expanded.

Despite this trend, however, there are thousands of rural churches in both village and country which are failing to make the necessary adaptations and which are therefore running into trouble. In many instances the churches themselves cannot be held responsible for failure to work out the needed adaptations, because they are confronted with social forces which are overwhelming in their magnitude and extremely difficult to meet. The open-country church, for example, is generally conceded by rural sociologists to be losing ground, for reasons quite similar to those which are causing the one-room schoolhouse and the open-country neighborhood recreation hall to recede, namely, a declining farm population, fewer and larger farms, year-round passable roads, and modern transportation facilities within the financial reach of nearly everyone. There is no reason to believe that the open-country church will disappear, but many of the marginal institutions, particularly those close to towns, have found their positions untenable.

While many rural churches have thus been unable to adapt themselves to the changing social situation through no fault of their own, there are some sister-institutions which are in difficulty because of a deliberate unwillingness to change or because of a reluctance to analyze their problems carefully and become aware of the possible solutions at hand.

There is a disturbing tendency in many small churches to confuse the essence of the religious institution with its outer manifestations and to safeguard the latter at the expense of the former. Take, for instance, the case of two quite similar churches in a hamlet, both of which have struggled for years to keep from succumbing. At best, the religious services offered by each are weak and minimal. If the two were combined under some reasonable arrangement, the economic base and the membership potential would be sufficient to establish one adequate program. But no! Both churches are protecting to the death their traditional administrative structures, at the obvious cost of the very work which they were originally dedicated to perform. They somehow do not realize that outward change may be essential to inner stability in a changing world.

Often, of course, such churches neglect to take necessary action because of unfamiliarity with the possible solutions at hand. In this chapter we shall try to outline briefly some of the steps which have been taken by many village and open-country churches to enrich and increase the adequacy of their religious programs. All approaches will not be pertinent to every institution, but most rural churches will probably derive benefit from evaluating their own situations in the light of the points raised.

Structural Reorganization

Some folks have the mistaken notion that reorganization is a panacea for the troubles of an ailing social group. "We must be set up wrong or we wouldn't be limping along the way we are!" Actually, the real source of weakness usually lies in the people themselves, in their lack of vision, inability to work together, or unwillingness to assume responsibility. Nevertheless, there are numerous instances in which the members of a rural church have fought a losing battle precisely because the structure of their institution was an obstacle to efficient operation. Regardless of how faithfully and cooperatively they worked, regardless of how much they sacrificed in time and money, they found their beloved little church losing ground.

Overchurching is a term commonly used to describe a situation in which the resources of a given area are insufficient to support adequately the number of churches which exist. Kolb and Brunner[1] point out that in 1936 "the average village-centered locality had 5.6 churches in the village itself and 3.6 churches in the open-country hinterland, a total of 9.2 churches for every community. . . ." Reflected in this statistic are many instances of overchurching. According to research conducted by H. P. Douglass, the problem seems to be most acute in the smallest places and in relatively poor counties. "Villages with less than 500 population have from two and a half to three times as many churches for each 1,000 persons as have large villages and towns."[2] Just how many churches can be adequately sup-

1. *Op. cit.*, p. 362.
2. *Ibid.*, p. 374.

ported in a given community will depend upon such factors, among others, as the socio-economic level of the people living there. It is clearly hazardous to generalize. As a rule-of-thumb, however, Douglas Ensminger states that "denominational leaders in the Home Mission Council say that to have strong churches the ratio should be one church for every thousand persons," whereas in rural communities today it is estimated that "there is one church for approximately every three hundred persons."[3]

Where overchurching exists, the only real alternative to continued emaciation and perhaps eventual extinction appears to lie in some form of structural organization under which the forces of hitherto independent churches are joined. Reorganization of this nature does not come easy for the rural church, because it often crosses denominational lines. Even where it does not, as in most Larger Parish arrangements where churches of only a single denomination are concerned, it requires that independent social structures yield to a new and broader framework which is designed to promote the welfare of all.

The Larger Parish is defined by Mark Rich as "a group of churches in a larger rural community, or a potential religious community, working together through a larger-parish council and a larger-parish staff to serve the people of the area with a diversified ministry."[4] Although there is no exact uniformity in structure among Larger Parishes throughout the country, they ordinarily involve a cooperative arrangement among several small churches of a given denomination (sometimes of various denominations) under which a staff of one or more ministers together with specialists in youth work, religious education, etc., function as a team under a parish council which is chosen by the member churches.

3. See Carl C. Taylor *et al., Rural Life in the United States* (New York: Alfred A. Knopf, 1949), p. 122.
4. See Mark Rich, *The Larger Parish* (Cornell Extension Bulletin, 1939).

Warren Corbett has described an interesting example, the Penn-Alpha Larger Parish, as follows:

On Sunday, March 29, 1953, nineteen new members were received into the membership of the New Lebanon, Pa., Presbyterian Church. This was an eventful day for this small church of sixty-eight members because not too long ago it was on the verge of being closed by the Presbytery. It received a new lease on life when it was included in the Penn-Alpha Larger Parish.

Penn-Alpha was formed by the Presbytery of Erie, Pennsylvania, in January, 1950, as the first Presbyterian larger parish in the Synod.

The Parish Council began to function in May of 1950. The early meetings were not always smooth because the [five] churches were not centrally located. Furthermore, they were fearful of losing their identities or of not getting their just share. This feeling has now been replaced by one of real effort and cooperation. . . .

The Parish Council and people worked together in creating a constitution. The Council, which meets quarterly, is composed of two representatives and two alternates from each church, one of each being a member of the Session. The Council's work is done through a program planning committee, a stewardship committee, and a youth council. The Moderator of the Council must be an ordained member of the staff. A volunteer children's worker and a voluntary secretary help to augment the efforts of the staff. . . .

Each church has its own women's and youth groups, and at one time ten choirs were operating in the Parish. Seventy per cent of the current income in the churches comes to the Parish treasury and meets all the expenses except local church upkeep and benevolences, which are cared for by each local church. . . .

We have a true Larger Parish: a Larger Parish Council, a written constitution, and a multiple diversified ministry. We have unified activities such as youth-week observances, a Sunday bulletin, Harvest Festival and Rural Life Sunday services, a music festival, Pentecost and Reformation services, an all-parish women's society and officers' training school, a common order of Sunday worship, joint vacation school planning, a larger parish treasury

> and budget; duplicating services; and joint ownership of audio-visual equipment and a filmstrip library.
>
> There people change slowly, but they are wonderful folks—"the salt of the earth." Cooperation is the only real hope of the small church. Betty Martin, the only clerk the Council has had, claims that the Parish has given the churches all of the advantages of the best city churches while they retain the friendliness of town and country churches.
>
> Words just can't explain all that we feel about the Larger Parish plan—its power and possibilities. One has to see to believe.[5]

The Federated Church is another form of church reorganization. This particular pattern unites "two or more local congregations of different denominations into one congregation" but provides for a retention of "membership in and all relationships with the parent denominations."[6] In a recent study,[7] a total of more than 600 unions of this type was found throughout the country, with the heaviest concentration occurring in the northeast and middle states. Most of the federations studied had been formed primarily for the purpose of keeping an "adequately supported pastor resident on the field," and were ordinarily organized only after the separate denominational approach had proved infeasible.

For the most part, the denominations involved had been reasonably successful in building a program of Christian education which drew upon materials from each group, but the pastors frequently reported difficulty in maintaining the "dual or triple denominational relationships" which were basic to the entire arrangement. In general, success appeared to be encouraged by a careful delineation of duties, responsibilities and rights in a

5. *Town and Country Church,* February, 1954, pp. 5-6. Published by the Department of Town and Country Church, Division of Home Missions, National Council of the Churches of Christ in the U.S.A.
6. Ralph L. Williamson, "Federated Churches," *Town and Country Church,* November, 1953, p. 1.
7. *Ibid.,* pp. 1, 2.

formal written agreement, by reliance upon educational methods, and by allowing sufficient time for the necessary psychological and legal adjustments to be made.

Other reorganizational patterns include "merging," "group ministry," "exchange of rights," and the "denominational" and "nondenominational" community churches. Space does not permit a description of each, but small rural churches which today are experiencing difficulty in providing an adequate program should be aware of the fact that hundreds of similar institutions throughout the nation have solved this very problem by working out some type of mutually satisfactory union.

A word of caution should be inserted here. Before proceeding too far with the development of any of the patterns noted above, the potentially cooperating church bodies should take time for a little research. The new church organization must be built upon a realistic factual foundation if it is to succeed. The congregations concerned need to take stock of their economic resources, local population trends, the legal aspects of union, and the many specific needs and problems which underlie their situation. If this is done they will know in advance exactly where they are going, and the chance of subsequent misunderstanding and unsuspected difficulties will be held to a minimum.

Technical advice is within easy reach of any group of churches contemplating a study of this nature. Letters to denominational headquarters, to national or state councils of churches, or to almost any state or private institution of higher learning will bring efficient and capable assistance.

Broadening the Program

It can be truthfully said of the average rural church that it does not make full use of the resources which are at its disposal. In this respect, of course, the rural church is not unique. Almost all of our social institutions could strengthen their programs immeasurably by more effective identification and utilization of existing resources.

In a recent study of 482 rural churches (92 per cent of the total of 526 rural churches in four Pennsylvania counties) Pennsylvania State College found that there were many improvements which might be made in the church programs concerned. "Many of them, particularly in the open country and small villages, did not have such activities as: organized groups for men or young people, choirs, 'church family nights,' lay leadership training classes, financial budgets, annual canvasses of members to support the budget, week-day religious education, and the like. Even such an elementary thing as regular church services at the same hour each Sunday was absent from many of the more rural churches."[8]

The heavy hand of custom has often precluded the birth of new ideas for the enrichment of religious experience in local congregations. Many a constructive proposal has been drowned in the well-known chorus: "It's never been done here before!" Every rural church should occasionally take a long and objective look at its past history. If no particular change of program has been evident, there is substantial reason to suspect that the church is in a rut. In a rural society which is changing as rapidly as ours, a static church program is cause for concern.

But what can a small church do to broaden and enrich its program? Perhaps the most fruitful approach is to scrutinize the wide variety of worthwhile activities carried on in other small churches, often at little or no extra expense, and to evaluate each as a possible addition to the local scene. Among these would be the following:

—a program of religious films.
—a series of family church nights.
—greater interest in soil conservation and closer cooperation with personnel of the Agricultural Extension Service.

8. "The Rural Churches of Four Pennsylvania Counties" (Progress Report No. 76, Agricultural Experiment Station, School of Agriculture, Pennsylvania State College, June, 1952).

—observance of Rural Life Sunday or a similar annual community festival.
—well-rounded programs for youth and for young adults.
—special attention to activities for the aged.
—book circle and discussion groups. Example: each of 24 families buys one new book annually, the books circulating among members of the group at two-week intervals; every month a meeting is held in some member's home, with a review and discussion of two of the books.
—an annual lecture-forum series.
—recreational programs for all age groups. For suggestions see "A Pastor Believes in Recreation," by E. O. Harbin, issued by the Department of General Church School Work, General Board of Education of the Methodist Church, 810 Broadway, Nashville 2, Tennessee; and "Planning Recreation for Rural Home and Community," Agricultural Information Bulletin No. 20, Superintendent of Documents, U. S. Government Printing Office, Washington 25, D. C. (30 cents).
—a leadership training program for laymen of the church, to strengthen participation in Sunday School and other activities.
—closer cooperation with community groups which are active in community improvement programs.
—greater emphasis upon town-and-country interdependence and upon the need for cooperative relationships.
—a good parish bulletin or paper.
—a systematic program for establishing contact with unchurched families and for welcoming new families.
—assistance to young families in their efforts to find suitable locations in the rural community.
—provision of literature on problems of the rural church to members of the congregation.
—a consistent program of visiting by the pastor, not limited to the death-bed or cases of serious illness.
—a counselling service by the pastor to young people who are planning to be married, or to anyone in the congregation who needs a helping hand.
—strengthening the worship service by less reliance on the notes for previous sermons and greater reliance on new religious ex-

periences through reading, conversation, and meditation as sources of inspiration for current messages from the pulpit.

In the forward-looking rural church, the pastor and his congregation are continuously on the alert for new ideas to strengthen their program. Only in this manner can adjustment be maintained with the changing world about them.

In-Service Training for Pastors and Laymen

During recent decades it has become increasingly clear to business and professional people throughout the nation that they dare not stop learning, even after the business place has been established or the shingle hung out. Whether one views it from the standpoint of keeping a step ahead of one's competitors or as a response to an inner urge for self-improvement, learning must go on. Changes are occurring in every area of human endeavor, and the man who makes no effort to keep abreast of new developments soon loses contact with his field. This is as true of the clergyman as of the doctor, lawyer, and business executive.

Much can be done through individual reading to make "lifelong learning" a reality. In addition to keeping in touch with literature in the field of religion itself, rural pastors and lay leaders will find identification with organizations such as the Adult Education Association of the U.S.A. a real help. (See page 110.) Its monthly publication, *Adult Leadership*, contains numerous articles which are directly relevant to the work of leaders in the rural parish. Note, for example, the following titles:

"Program Resources for the Holiday [Christmas] Season"
"How to Plan and Run a Conference"
"The Meaning of Community Leadership"
"Some Essentials of International Understanding"
"Newcomers in Our Midst"
"Building Committees that Work"
"Are Goals Worth While?"

While substantial self-improvement is possible through consistent reading of periodicals, pamphlets and books, there are additional benefits which can be derived only from personal contact with kindred souls. The writings of a great religious leader ordinarily take on new meaning for the local pastor who has an opportunity actually to hear him speak or to visit with him informally. Further, the pastor who finds it possible to spend a few days each year sharing experiences with other clergymen, getting new ideas from them and enjoying the fellowship which only such association can bring will find himself well repaid for the time and money invested.

Such experiences are readily available to rural religious leaders through institutes and short courses offered in almost all parts of the United States. Benson Y. Landis has pointed out that there "are said to be 200 places where a country priest or a country minister may go for refresher courses, mainly during the summer months,"[9] but certainly also at other times of the year. A few cases will serve to illustrate the wealth of opportunities which exist for education, inspiration, and fellowship.

Well known to Protestant denominations are the annual "Town and Country Church" conferences which are held on the campuses of Land Grant colleges in many states. These exert a strong influence toward helping rural church leaders visualize and understand the church as an integral part of the rural social scene. Excellent annual conferences are also conducted by state councils of churches and by many individual denominational bodies.

The 1954 Annual Nebraska Ministers' Convocation, sponsored by the Nebraska Council of Churches, included a School for Pastors which provided for three intensive sessions on each of the following subjects: "Church History and the Ecumenical Movement," "Christ, the Hope of the World" (theme of the 1954 Assembly of the World Council of Churches), "A Community Approach to Evangelism," "Worship and the Devotional

9. *Town and Country Church,* October, 1953, p. 12.

Life," "The World Mission of the Church," and "Community Problems." Among the leaders were such national figures as Dr. Halford E. Luccock and Dr. Henry Smith Leiper, as well as rural sociologists and economists from the staff of the University of Nebraska. It is difficult to see how a rural pastor can go wrong in attending meetings of this quality.

A specialized type of rural institute on Church Music and Worship was sponsored by the Virginia Council of Churches in Pittsylvania County. This institute was designed primarily for "choir directors, organists, pianists, choir members, ministers and church school leaders." Its purpose was "to provide an opportunity for church workers of all denominations to study principles and methods of improving the music and worship services of the local rural church." In the words of Henry Langford, the institute "showed that small country churches may, by correct planning and diligent study, have a church service that is just as worshipful and impressive as that held in any large city church."[10]

Another promising development is found in the county one-day institutes which bring religious leaders, professional people from various public service agencies, and leaders of many types of community organizations together. More than one hundred such meetings have been held in Virginia under the name "Interdenominational County Rural Life Institute," conducted jointly by the Agricultural Extension Service, the ministers of interested denominations, and the representatives of other community groups.

The following benefits have been observed from these county institutes in Virginia: the ministers "have received new insights concerning the effects of the economic, social, and cultural environment upon rural life, rural people, and the rural church"; the professional workers and other community leaders have gained "a new appreciation of the Church and the religious

10. See Henry Langford, "Rural Institute on Church Music and Worship," *Town and Country Church,* March, 1952, p. 9.

values of their own work"; and all participants together have attained a higher degree of mutual understanding.[11]

Richard O. Comfort has made a number of special studies of training programs offered for the rural ministry in the United States. He concludes that the following "ten characteristics of a good rural minister" seem to stand out. The good rural minister should:

> have a sound personal religion. . . .
> understand rural life and be consecrated to it. . . .
> identify himself with the people he serves but . . . also constantly try to help them aspire to higher things. . . .
> be adaptable, versatile and have a lot of patience. . . .
> be aware of the "county seat" and the resources to be found there, such as the welfare department, the county agricultural agent, and others. . . .
> understand the needs of the young people. . . .
> develop a Christian recreation program where it is needed. . . .
> be aware of the various social institutions and of their need of the ministry. . . .
> know how to use the limited resources to produce maximum results. . . .
> love rural people . . . [and] not think of his task as a sacrifice.[12]

Assuming that these criteria of a good rural minister are reasonably accurate, it would seem that any pastor who considers his education completed upon graduation from a seminary is destined to be somewhat less than mediocre in his service to the congregations which he will serve. A significant phase of the rural pastor's education begins as he enters his first pulpit, and the institute in all its various forms is one of his great resources in this in-service training process.

Participation of rural religious leaders in educational programs

11. C. Ralph Arthur, "Interdenominational County Rural Life Institutes in Virginia," *Town and Country Church*, February, 1953, p. 12.
12. Richard O. Comfort, "The Training of the Rural Ministry," *Town and Country Church*, December, 1952, pp. 1-2.

of this nature is far below what it should be because, in large measure, of the failure of the leaders themselves to appreciate the benefits to be derived. Occasionally, however, the congregation is at fault—where, for example, a minister is made to understand that he is not being paid to "go gallivanting around to meetings!" It is in the best interests of every congregation to have its minister, and if possible some of its lay leaders, attend at least one good conference or institute annually.

Interfaith Cooperation

It is paradoxical that the social institutions most clearly dedicated to the ideals of love and human brotherhood in our society should so widely have exemplified exactly the opposite values in their relationships with each other. Religious wars have been fought—with the "sword" in the international arena and with the no less deadly "word" on the home front. And even where the heat of actual conflict has not been found, a spirit of deliberate non-cooperation has often chilled the social atmosphere. Religious strife is particularly unfortunate when one considers the powerful forces of evil which seem to be omnipresent in our world. With so much work to be done in combatting these forces, it is regrettable that our churches should have devoted so much time and effort through the years to fighting among themselves—or to ignoring each other.

Recently a much-dejected minister described to the author a disturbing incident which he had just experienced. He was one of several pastors appointed to a committee whose task it was to work out solutions to a number of welfare problems having certain religious implications. All committee members belonged to various branches of the same Protestant denomination. At a lull in the deliberations of the committee on that day, one of the members produced a letter from his church headquarters stating that it would be necessary for him to withdraw from the committee unless the opening prayer could be omitted from the agenda of future meetings. . . . Our dejected friend wondered: "How can the church possibly become an important influence for world peace and understanding if a handful of spiritual leaders from the same broad denomination can't even share with each other the experience of prayer?"

In this sixth decade of the twentieth century we have a long road to travel before the goal of full cooperation among religious bodies is attained. Despite many such disheartening situations as the above, however, there are hopeful signs on the horizon. The rural community has a tremendous stake in the ultimate realization of this goal because nowhere can religious cleavage do more to destroy the sense of community than here.

Let us note a few of the developments which augur well for the future. Some years ago the leaders of the National Catholic Rural Life Conference and the Rural Life Association completed the formation of a National Committee on Religion and Rural Life. Its stated purpose is "to stimulate, encourage and allocate funds toward the support of, and to unite in common cause, Catholic, Protestant and other groups, agencies and persons, which are striving to achieve a deeper and more significant appreciation of the spiritual values in rural life by conducting and sponsoring educational programs and projects and activities emphasizing the values, needs and opportunities of rural living and the religious basis for the conservation and development of spiritual, human and natural resources in rural areas." The National Committee will use its financial resources "to aid special surveys, projects and studies relating to religion and rural life, on a non-denominational basis" and the "chairman of the board will be appointed alternately by Catholics and Protestants."[13]

Since it was founded in 1928, the National Conference of Christians and Jews has been an important influence toward interfaith cooperation in the United States. The N.C.C.J. describes itself as "a civic organization of religiously motivated persons to promote justice, amity, understanding and coopera-

13. *Town and Country Church,* October, 1952, p. 15.

tion among Protestants, Catholics and Jews. It does not aim at any sort of union or amalgamation of religious bodies or at modifying any of the distinctive beliefs of its members. It does not attempt to achieve its goal by weakening the loyalties and beliefs of those of any religion. It does not hold that 'one religion is as good as another.' "[14]

Through 62 offices in cities from coast to coast, it has developed a broad program to combat bigotry and hate by "stressing the moral content of democracy." It "works to keep prejudice out of our schools . . . provides an instrument whereby ministers, priests and rabbis and their congregations can join in the crusade for brotherhood . . . works with fraternal, civic, welfare, labor, veteran, women's and youth organizations to help make democratic good will a pattern of American living in every neighborhood . . . has developed an in-plant program to promote good human relations within plants and factories . . . in a nationwide campaign against bigotry, it has enlisted the co-operation of newspapers, radio, television, motion pictures, advertising, magazines, books, pamphlets, speakers and recordings." Since 1934 the N.C.C.J. has sponsored the annual observance of Brotherhood Week.

The National Council of the Churches of Christ in the U.S.A. is a fellowship of thirty nation-wide denominations "representing most of the major historic bodies of American Christianity, except the Roman Catholic. These include Baptists, Brethren, Congregationalists, Disciples, Eastern Orthodox, Episcopalians, Evangelical United Brethren, Friends, Lutherans, Methodists, Moravians, Presbyterians, Reformed, and others. . . . It rejects all thought of enforced uniformity. It seeks only the kind of unity which is consistent with liberty and diversity. As leaders of the churches meet and work together they find that the Christian convictions and interests which they have in common are far more important than their differences. They

14. "Lighting Lamps." Published by the National Conference of Christians and Jews, 381 Fourth Avenue, New York 16, N. Y.

also discover that cooperation does not require any church to relinquish any part of its own historic heritage."[15]

The National Council of Churches has four main divisions: Home Missions, Foreign Missions, Christian Education, and Christian Life and Work. Through these it conducts a broad cooperative program, illustrated by specific united projects such as the following:

publishing the Revised Standard Version of the Bible;
completing the resettlement of displaced persons in new homes;
presenting Christian messages on radio and television networks (1,667 different programs in 1952);
providing a "ministry-on-wheels" to migrant workers;
teaching illiterates around the world to read;
helping local communities to organize councils of churches;
maintaining and extending concrete projects to improve relations between races and nations.

The work of this Council is financed primarily through direct contributions from the member churches, gifts from individuals, and appropriations by foundations, corporations and other organizations. Its Operations Budget for 1953 was $7,838,044.

Hopeful developments on the interdenominational front are by no means limited to programs related to organization such as the above. In local communities there are numerous ways in which diverse religious bodies cooperate to achieve common goals. There are joint Easter sunrise services, musical programs, lecture series, social gatherings, and summer church-school programs, in addition to many types of united activities within civic organizations such as community councils. The sphere of cooperative effort among our many religious bodies is still regrettably small, but it is growing.

15. "The National Council of Churches. What Is It? What Does It Do?" Published by the National Council of the Churches of Christ in the U.S.A., 297 Fourth Avenue, New York 10, N. Y.

11

LOCAL GOVERNMENT

. . . that government of the people, by the people, for the people, shall not perish from the earth.—GETTYSBURG ADDRESS

IT IS UNDOUBTEDLY A MISTAKE to look upon these words of Abraham Lincoln as pertaining only to the war which was fought among American brothers nearly a century ago. They are far more than that. Through them, a message has resounded to all succeeding generations that government must remain closely integrated with the people.

This message appears doubly significant today because so large a portion of the world's population lives under circumstances where governmental power is quite unrelated to the public will. Positions of control are obtained by violent means and maintained through ruthless suppression of those who have the courage to dissent. Social patterns are dictated from above, and outward conformity is made to prevail regardless of inner conviction. Governmental decrees are based upon public opinion only if the latter happens to coincide with the will of the ruling minority.

Among the most effective safeguards against this state of affairs is a vigorous participation in local government by citizens throughout the land. Failure to utilize fully the democratic processes which are at hand leads to gradual disintegration of what we proudly refer to as "the American way," and where such disintegration occurs, the authoritarian pattern is readily imposed.

Example are plentiful in the history of American government to show that bosses, selfish minority groups, and cliques are prepared to take advantage of any laxity on the part of local citizens in the exercise of their democratic duties and rights. The names of Tweed, Pendergast, and others like them have been written in large, dark letters across the urban American scene, but their kind are by no means confined to cities. Illustrations, equally dramatic though on a smaller scale, can be drawn from many rural areas where "the courthouse gang," as referred to by Lancaster,[1] has exploited the public for selfish purposes. One reason for such exploitation lies in the apathy of the voting public. It could not occur if people really wanted to prevent it.

Rural governmental problems will be examined here under three general headings. The first has to do with structure, the second with personnel, and the third with the relation of the rural environment to law enforcement.

Structure

Students of political science have pointed out that rural government in the United States suffers from a malady known as cultural lag. This term refers to the tendency of actual social conditions to change more rapidly than society's methods of dealing with them, thus causing social maladjustment. Techniques and structures persist into the modern era which may have been well adapted to meeting the needs of an earlier day but which prove impotent in the face of the contemporary social situation.

At a recent session of the community club in a small locality, a township officer who was planning to withdraw from his post on the township board made the following com-

1. Lane W. Lancaster, *Government in Rural America,* 2nd ed. (New York: D. Van Nostrand Co., Inc., 1952), p. 57.

ment: "Now, listen, fellas! The annual meeting of our township is coming up right soon, and I'm planning to decline re-election. I think I've done my share, and I want you men to be present at the meeting so that someone else can be elected to take my place. At recent annual meetings we have not had more than one or two people present besides the officers, and this is bad business!"

To some extent the difficulty in this township was indifference on the part of the voters. Even more significant, however, was the probability that the township form of government had outlived its usefulness there, as in many other parts of the United States, and was now limping along on a "one or two participants" basis. Lancaster states: "The vast majority of townships are condemned on every count. They are lacking in social unity, too small in area and population, and too weak in taxable resources to become vigorous units of government. There is not a function performed by the township which could not be better performed by other units. And in fact it is being slowly starved to death. The county and state are stripping it of such functions as the care of roads, poor relief, and public health, while the incorporation of villages and small cities has depleted very seriously its taxable resources."[2] As is so frequently the case, the outer framework tends to remain intact for years after new social conditions have indicated that a change is in order.

The township is not the only rural governmental unit which gives evidence of lag. Many of the rural counties of the United States are carrying needlessly large overhead expenses which could be notably lessened through some type of county consolidation. A prominent factor in the original determination of county boundaries was the distance that a team of horses could travel in a day. Today this factor is irrelevant, and we have far more county seats (complete with buildings, equipment, and personnel) than are actually needed in the light of our present mile-a-minute speeds on public highways.

The citizens of county seats in many rural areas would proba-

2. *Ibid.*, p. 67.

bly agree that the economy and efficiency of county government could be enhanced by the development of larger units commensurate with modern transportation facilities. But trouble arises when attention is turned to the problem of determining which municipalities shall prevail as the county seats and which shall revert to the status of non-county seat towns. To this day, there are open wounds from vicious battles which were fought among towns over the original location of county seats. The probable recurrence of such fights is a major deterrent to any serious step toward bringing the structure of county governments into conformity with current logical possibilities.

The village also has the problem of keeping itself structurally adapted to a changing world. One aspect thereof was voiced by Anderson and Miller: "Increasingly the rural town is becoming the focus of social institutions in the farm community, although the farmer-citizen is limited by traditional patterns of local government, school districts, and so on. A critical factor in village survival and adjustment may be the degree to which there is informal consultation if not equal legal participation among farm and town people on decisions that concern the whole community. The downward adjustment of farm population to land resources calls for corresponding adjustment of institutions and rural communities."[3]

Such readjustment is already under way in certain rural institutional fields. The waning of the open-country church was noted in the previous chapter. Where this institution closes its doors, however, the people concerned are not thereby deprived of religious services. They obtain them in a presumably better and more complete form in village churches which adapt themselves to make provision for the influx from farm areas. The new members from the open country become fully integrated with these churches and are eligible to assume positions of authority within the institutional structures on the same basis as village residents.

3. *Op. cit.*, p. 27.

To a lesser degree, the same is true of the patrons of small open-country schools which are discontinued in favor of larger central schools. Where the shift of pupils from an open country to a village school is accompanied by appropriate reorganization of school districts, the farm children are not considered outsiders and their parents have a legal voice in the determination of school policies. Where such reorganization of districts does not occur the farm children ordinarily attend the village school under some sort of special tuition or contract arrangement, and their parents have no right to vote on school matters. This is at best a temporary makeshift, looking forward to the day when all families who have children in a school will also be entitled to a voice in its affairs.

In village government the lag is far more widespread. Over a period of many years the open-country population has become more and more closely identified with village affairs. No longer is the farmer a person who occasionally goes to town to do his shopping. On an increasing scale, he makes almost daily appearances for a wide variety of activities. He is directly concerned with the many services and facilities provided by village government: streets, lighting systems, water supply, public restrooms, parks and recreational areas, inspection of food handlers, and so on. He benefits greatly from these provisions of municipal government but does not help to support them financially, at least directly, nor does he have any voice at all in their direction.

The day is probably still distant when the *sociological community* (town and farm as a unified whole) will attain legal and political status, but the handwriting is on the wall. Boundary lines separating town and farm are becoming more obscure as the rural community approaches an ever-higher degree of integration. It is reasonable to assume that this social system may eventually evolve to the point where the farm population not only belongs to the community informally but is a part of its formal political structure as well. In the meantime, serious attention must be given to increasing the amount of joint action among farm and town people on matters of community-wide concern, as indicated by Anderson and Miller above.

Underlying many of the governmental problems in rural areas is the crazy-quilt structural pattern of local administrative units. According to U.S. Census figures for 1942 there were 155,116 governmental units in the United States, including 3,050 counties, 18,919 towns and townships, 3,332 urban municipalities, 12,888 rural municipalities, 108,579 school districts, and 8,299 special districts. In reference to this situation, Kolb and Brunner point out that the "large number of units, their wide distribution among counties, townships, municipalities, and school and other special districts, and their inter-relations, present a puzzling picture to the uninitiated and often to the professional as well. The distribution of all types of units follows no definite rule either as to population served, extent of areas covered, or taxable base for support."[4]

Here is a situation where confusion and inefficiency are almost inherent and where frustration is a natural end-product for the conscientious voter. "A locality in the East was found to have eleven different elections each year, some on the township basis, but the majority on the special district basis. Apparently under many local conditions it is easier to organize a special district for a special purpose than it is to reorganize existing units to perform new duties."[5]

In general, the trend is toward fewer local governmental units, but the problem ahead is still complex. While townships are being liquidated upon assumption of their traditional duties by larger units, and while the number of school districts is dropping noticeably through consolidations, there are new needs which seem to call for the creation of additional special districts from time to time. Illustrative of the latter is the vast network

4. *Op. cit.*, p. 459.
5. *Ibid.*, p. 461.

of soil conservation districts designed to promote conservation practices on agricultural lands.

A reduction in the number of local governmental units is not an end in itself. Each type of unit must be judged on its merits. The goal is an efficient over-all structure which operates at reasonable cost and facilitates intelligent participation by the general public.

Personnel

Sound structure is essential to good government. Even more important is well-trained and efficient personnel, devoted to the public welfare. Through the years, the small community has encountered difficulty in obtaining public servants of high calibre. This has been due partly to the ease with which self-centered candidates have found it possible to gain votes from an unsuspecting and easy-going electorate, partly to the difficulty of encouraging good men to run for public office, and partly to the fact that even the most socially desirable office-holders ordinarily have no way of securing special training for their governmental tasks.

In regard to local rural government, Lancaster believes that there is "no greater need today than the creation of an able public service which, guaranteed security, adequate salary, and social esteem, may safely be entrusted with the management of the public business."[6] Our concern here is with the question of what can be done to help conscientious local officials become an "able public service."

It is little short of amazing how feeble our public concern is toward the training of local governmental officials. A casual look at the business world reveals all sorts of orientation and training programs which are provided for new employees, to say nothing of their seasoned co-workers. Every graduate of a medical college is given a period of intensive internship before he is permitted to open a practice. Every adequate curriculum

6. *Op. cit.*, p. 89.

for the education of teachers includes practice teaching under capable supervision. Most students of theology have had at least a modicum of practical experience in the pulpit before accepting the first call.

The procedure is quite different, however, where people are chosen for public office. . . . A man takes a notion that he wants to be sheriff, conducts a successful campaign, has a badge pinned on his jacket, and goes to work. Ordinarily, he becomes familiar with the intricacies of his job by a process of trial and error, at the public's expense. . . . A housewife looking for a chance to earn a little extra pocket money applies for the job of assessor and without further ado is assigned the highly technical task of evaluating local property for taxation purposes. . . . A local citizen is elected mayor of a village and assumes the leadership of its governmental activities without any type of training for his post except what he may have picked up by chance along the way. Regardless of how small the town may be, the problems which come to him and his co-workers for decision are often of such a nature that mistakes can be very costly to the general public. To function effectively as a mayor, he needs a rather clear understanding of the role of local government and its relation to other governmental units. He needs, in addition, certain skills which are essential to the efficient operation of the business affairs of his locality. The need for help in gaining a basic orientation to this job is reflected in a letter which was recently received by the president of a state university from a small-town mayor:

Dear Sir:

I would like to have a few books on Duties of Mayors and also of Marshals in small towns like ———. Also I would like to have a couple of Town Marshal badges.

Has the Mayor got the right to deputize anyone to help the Marshal?

Yours truly,

————————, Mayor.

Yes, there are books and manuals to which this mayor and other rural governmental officials like him can turn for guidance, but often these are written in language that is difficult to comprehend. Further, the mere reading of reference books provides, at best, a limited type of orientation. Lacking is the opportunity to discuss troublesome points with people who are well informed.

The Institute of Government at the University of North Carolina is perhaps the best-known example of a well-rounded program established to meet the urgent need for the training of governmental officials. With regard to the problem of bridging the gap between outgoing and incoming public officials in North Carolina, Albert Coates, as the Institute director, commented as follows:

> Every two or four years hosts of newly elected officials come into the administration of public affairs. . . . These officials are not born with a knowledge of the powers and duties of the offices to which they are elected—the office of sheriff or chief of police, clerk of court or register of deeds, city alderman or county commissioner. Their private occupations and professions do not teach them the powers and duties of public officials. The uncertainties of political life do not offer them incentives to study the responsibilities of a public office before they seek it. The democracy which clothes them with the public trust does not provide them with the training which fits them to discharge it.
>
> They go into office to learn by mistakes which might have been avoided, in the school of hard knocks which sometimes knock harder on the public than on the public officer. The learning they acquire in this rough, ready and expensive fashion too often goes out of office with them at the end of their official terms.[7]

To remedy this situation a program was developed which provided, first, for a series of comparative studies in criminal law administration, tax administration, accounting and finance,

7. Albert Coates, "The Story of the Institute of Government," p. 15. Published by the National University Extension Association, University of Indiana, Bloomington, 1944.

public health, public welfare, federal-state-local relationships, and other pertinent subject areas. Through these studies a valuable store of practical information was gained regarding laws and governmental operations at the various levels in North Carolina. These materials were compiled into a series of guidebooks written "simply and concretely enough for any person with common sense to read and understand."[8]

Training schools were then established for the various types of governmental officials. Some of these were held on a statewide basis; others were conducted in districts; and still others, in local communities. These schools were supplemented by a clearing house of helpful information and by a "governmental laboratory" designed to demonstrate in a practical manner the fundamental processes of good government.

Similar programs for the training of governmental officials exist in various other states, but most of them are on a markedly smaller scale. If the quality of public service characteristic of rural America is to be improved, this type of adult-education activity must be greatly expanded. In the meantime the people of our smaller communities do not need to sit idly by, waiting for such programs to be developed for them. Adult-education activities are generated in rather direct proportion to the demands which become apparent. If the small community will clarify its own thinking in this regard and make its wishes for training programs known, the day will not be distant when our institutions of higher learning and other public agencies will move strongly in this direction.

Rural Environment and Law Enforcement

One of the most satisfying features of life in the small community is the close personal relationship which exists among its people. It provides a sense of community which cannot be found in the larger urban areas. With regard to law enforce-

8. *Ibid.*, p. 20.

ment, however, this type of relationship often proves to be a complicating factor.

Effective law enforcement requires objectivity on the part of the enforcing officer, whose responsibility it is to act promptly and impartially wherever violations occur. The difficulty of his task is closely related to the number and the closeness of the personal bonds which tie him to the people whom he serves. It is more difficult to issue a ticket for an illegal U-turn on Main Street to one of his kinfolks, to an elder of his church, to a fellow Legionnaire, to a golf companion, or to the teen-age son of an influential local citizen than to a person with whom he has no personal relationship whatever. In the average small community the local peace officer is more or less personally acquainted with most of the persons who come under his jurisdiction, and the typical situation which calls for official action causes him some degree of emotional concern.

To remedy this situation some towns have followed the practice of hiring a comparative stranger from another locality, the assumption being that for a while at least he will be unfettered in his official functions. In one village of about 1,200 population where this was done, the newly appointed constable found a car astride a parking stripe one Saturday evening. As he was making out the ticket, a lady approached the car and unloaded an armful of groceries in the front seat. Upon sizing up the situation, she registered a protest and asked in a firm tone of voice: "Do you know who I am?" Receiving a negative reply, she added, "I'm Mrs. ——!" (the local banker's wife), to which the constable calmly responded, "Lady, I don't care *who* you are! You are parked wrong and it's my duty to give you this ticket."

Another approach to this problem lies in the further professionalization of local law enforcement officers. The small community can probably never aspire to having peace officers who have received training comparable to that of their urban counterparts, but much can be done through taking advantage of adult-education opportunities which are available. A local rural officer who has had the benefit of a short course or two in law enforcement will be strengthened, not only by having acquired a greater know-how in relation to his duties, but also by a feeling of professional status that naturally comes with scientific training.

A further example of the enforcement complications inherent in the small town's personal atmosphere may be cited from a village of 300 population where the town board had decided to grade and place crushed rock on a number of dirt alleys. As the street crew went to work they came upon a well-known elderly gentleman who had planted his vegetable garden in the alley and who was utterly out of sympathy with the project under way. Legally, an alley is no place for a garden, whether it be in a hamlet or metropolis, but rural authorities confronted with situations such as the above are in a more difficult position than their counterparts in urban areas. Personal sentiment, an obstacle not easily overcome, sometimes leads to delay or even abandonment of needed improvements.

Rural zoning provides another case in point. In the words of Louis A. Wolfanger, "One of the . . . problems confronting many villages is the growth of 'home occupations' or businesses in the residence areas. One neighbor starts dismantling old motor vehicles in his backyard and selling the parts. Another saws and hammers at late hours making furniture. Another runs a welding shop in his garage. Another raises rabbits, or pigeons, or blooded dogs. . . . It is generally admitted . . . that such occupations will in time break down the residential quality of a neighborhood if continued and expanded."[9]

Among the major objections to zoning, as voiced in rural Michigan areas, are the following: "Zoning is dictatorship"; "I have the right to use my property as I please!"; "We have

9. "What is Happening in *Your* Community?" (Rural Zoning Leaflet No. 1, Preliminary Draft, Department of Land and Water Conservation, Michigan State College), p. 8.

too many laws now!"; "We don't need zoning"; "Zoning hurts property values"; and "Zoning will increase taxes."[10] The answers to such objections are obvious to anyone who is familiar with the zoning concept, particularly if it is his neighbor's land which is being utilized for socially distasteful purposes.

It is true of both rural and urban communities that there is a place for everything and everything should be in its place! In cities this principle is now well established, although serious administrative problems exist in many localities, due partially to the constant pressure upon the authorities for exceptions to the zoning regulations. In rural areas throughout the nation the zoning idea has not made much headway to date. With the present growing emphasis upon community improvement the idea is probably destined to take root, but the highly personalized relationships of the small community must be recognized as a major deterrent.

As one small-town businessman expressed it to the author: "Yes, we have a zoning ordinance in our village, but it's now a dead letter. I was in on the enforcing end of it for a while, but believe you me, that's the last time I'll ever try anything like that!" As a zoning official he had made his decisions in a firm, objective manner, but he was utterly dismayed at the repercussions which arose from his official actions—often of highly personal significance to himself and his family. He could not make his decisions and then forget about them. They came home to roost through the intricate network of personal relationships which characterize and affect almost every phase of human living in the small community.

Ultimate improvement in relation to this aspect of law enforcement in rural areas lies in the development of a more mature citizenry. People must come to realize that the entire

10. Louis A. Wolfanger, "I'm for Zoning!—I'm Against Zoning!" (Rural Zoning Leaflet No. 3, Preliminary Draft, Michigan State College), pp. 4-10.

community suffers when local public officials who are courageous enough to perform their assigned duties are faced with a constant danger of reprisal. The latter leads inevitably to mediocrity and inaction in public office.

12

MEDICAL CARE

Work, and the health to do it, are the greatest blessings God gives to mankind.—PEARLEY

SIGNIFICANT PROGRESS has been made in the United States toward erasing inequalities between rural and urban levels of living, but the job of equalization is far from ended. Among the areas which still need serious attention is that of medical care. In the very nature of the case, there can never be full equality in the accessibility of medical care to rural and urban residents, but we do have a right to look forward to the day when there will be an over-all pattern of rural-urban service which meets the needs of all. Every farm and small-town family should have easy access to a well-trained physician and reasonable access to such hospital facilities and specialists as are needed.

An indication of the problems confronting rural areas today is found in a popularly written bulletin entitled "What Has Happened to the Country Doctor?" by John H. Lane, Jr.[1] The author points out that in Missouri

> a decline in the number of physicians has continued for the last forty years. During this period the state has suffered a net loss of about 1,000 doctors—from more than 6,000 in 1912 to about

1. Bulletin 594, Agricultural Experiment Station, College of Agriculture, University of Missouri, February, 1953. See p. 5.

> 5,000 today. But the loss is far greater than these figures show. For during this same 40-year period Missouri had a population increase of more than 600,000 persons.
>
> The rural areas of the state have been particularly hard hit by the decline in number of doctors. A recent survey of physician supply in twenty Missouri counties, most of which are rural (having no towns over 2,500 population), reveals a drastic change in number of physicians. In 1912, a total of 539 physicians resided in the 20-county area; in 1950, there were only 158. This represents a loss of about 70 per cent during the last forty years. Furthermore, the greatest percentage loss has taken place during the last ten years. Since 1940, the 20-county area has lost more than one-third of its doctors.

Areas of this nature may not be typical of all rural America, but their situation is disturbing and hardly unique.[2]

On the national scene we find that doctors in rural areas have been growing "progressively fewer and older" since the turn of the century.[3] The generally accepted maximum ratio of population to doctors is 1,500:1. To exceed this figure is to threaten the adequacy of medical care. In the United States as a whole there was in 1940 "about one physician for every 800 persons. In cities, however, there were only 580 people per doctor as compared with 1,336 in rural areas. Nearly 11 million people are living in more than one thousand of the nation's most rural counties, in which there is only one physician for every 1,700 persons. When calculations are made to take into account the effects of age upon these doctors, the ratio is in-

2. A pertinent regional study, sponsored by the Health Committee of the Northern Great Plains Council, was published in 1954 by the Agricultural Experiment Station, University of Nebraska, at Lincoln: "Health Resources in the Northern Great Plains," by A. H. Anderson, U. S. Bureau of Agricultural Economics. This publication gives information about health facilities and professional personnel in the 399 counties of six states, and about state agencies and organizations concerned with health. It discusses the problems of rural communities in this important field.
3. Loomis and Beegle, *op. cit.*, p. 716.

creased to one to 1,964. With this adjustment, New Mexico, with a ratio of one 'effective' physician per 3,738 persons, makes the poorest showing."[4]

The scarcity of dentists in rural communities is also well known, at least among rural people. Ensminger and Longmore point out that "while no difference in the amount of dental care appears between the large and small cities, the rate (annual dental cases per 1,000 population) for rural areas is about half that of cities over 5,000 population.[5]

Turning to the field of nursing, we find a generally similar picture. In 1940 the rural people of the United States (rural-farm and rural-nonfarm) constituted 43.5 per cent of our total population but could boast only 14.5 per cent of the total employed trained nurses and student nurses.[6]

Regarding facilities available for care of the mentally ill, the Commission on Hospital Care[7] stated that "probably no single type of institutional care is so lacking in competent and sufficient personnel as are the nervous and mental hospitals throughout the country." The Commission presented statistical evidence to show that the number of beds per 1,000 population in hospitals for mental diseases in the year 1945 was substantially lower in those states of the South and West which were largely rural than in most other parts of the United States. Loomis and Beegle add that "rural areas are practically without professional services for mental sickness."[8]

4. *Ibid.*, pp. 716-17. See also *Report to the Committee on Education and Labor* (Senate Committee Print No. 4, Government Printing Office, 1946), p. 16; and F. D. Mott and M. I. Roemer, *Rural Health and Medical Care* (New York: McGraw-Hill Book Co., 1948), p. 151.
5. Taylor *et al., op. cit.,* p. 165.
6. Loomis and Beegle, *op. cit.,* p. 712.
7. Commission on Hospital Care, *Hospital Care in the United States* (New York: The Commonwealth Fund, 1947). See Loomis and Beegle, *op. cit.,* pp. 739, 741.
8. *Op. cit.,* p. 739.

Finally, it must be conceded that rural areas do not compare favorably with urban in relation to public health services designed for the prevention of disease. Mott and Roemer have gathered data showing that rural people are at a disadvantage when compared with urban people in regard to services rendered by public health agencies.[9]

THE ROAD AHEAD

In viewing unpleasant facts such as the foregoing, one is tempted to look for a scapegoat. There must be someone who can be blamed for the deficiencies of medical care in rural America! Actually, the causes are complex, and nothing whatever is gained by trying to pin responsibility for the situation upon anyone, including the newly graduated M.D. who decides to hang up his shingle in a city instead of accepting an invitation from a rural community. The explanation for his decision lies in a social situation rather than in stubbornness or selfishness on his part, and it is through a careful study of such social situations that we shall eventually be able to devise an effective solution.

During recent years a number of developments have occurred which hold real promise for the future. A few of the more significant ones will be reviewed briefly here.

Provision of Physical Facilities by the Community. Some years ago Dr. Franklin D. Murphy, dean of the Medical Center at the University of Kansas, was seriously perturbed at the shortage of general medical practitioners in the rural communities of his state. In seeking an explanation of why the graduates of his own institution did not practice to any appreciable extent in rural areas, he called upon his junior and senior medical students and "asked a blunt question: 'Why won't you fellows take up general practice in a small town?' The replies were revealing. Most graduates, heavily in debt after years in medical school, could not afford to practice the way they had been

9. See Mott and Roemer, *op. cit.*, pp. 348, 349.

taught. Up-to-date equipment alone costs up to $10,000. It was more practical—and much simpler—to share the office of a well-established metropolitan doctor. There was a second reason: students feared 'medical isolation' if they settled in small communities. None wanted to be cut off from news of medical advances."[10] With this valuable information in hand, the University of Kansas developed a program which has gained national recognition as an intelligent and practical approach to the problem.

The first objection to medical practice in rural areas, namely, the lack of physical facilities for the young M.D., was counteracted by helping rural Kansans see that their chances of getting and holding a doctor would be enhanced by providing just such facilities. As a result, a substantial number of small communities, or community organizations, took it upon themselves to raise funds for the construction of clinics or doctors' offices with appropriate equipment which could be sold on easy terms or rented at low cost to any acceptable physician who became interested. The effectiveness of this approach is confirmed not only by the experience of Kansas to date, but by that of many other states which are experimenting along similar lines.

Among the projects with which the writer is personally familiar was that in Ceresco, Nebraska, a village of 374 people. Here a crisis arose during the spring of 1951, when Dr. W. W. Noyes, who had served the community for nearly thirty years, suffered a heart attack sufficiently severe to convince him that he should no longer climb the flight of stairs to his office above the local drug store. In addition, the veteran M. D. was approaching three score and ten and the Ceresco folks felt that his eventual retirement might leave them in a difficult predicament. The problem was therefore to provide Dr. Noyes with an office on the ground floor as long as he continued to practice,

10. Alvin S. McCoy and Ralph H. Major, Jr., "Kansas Answers 'Socialized Medicine.'" Reprinted from *Coronet,* September, 1949; copyright 1949 by Esquire, Inc.

and to create facilities which would be adequate to attract a successor upon his retirement.

At this point the Ceresco Commercial Club went to work. After studying reports on pertinent projects in Kansas and tapping various sources of information, including the University of Nebraska, a decision was reached. The Commercial Club, an incorporated body, would spearhead a drive to raise funds and volunteer labor for the construction of a Community Health Clinic. Title to the new property would be held by the Commercial Club as the most practical arrangement, and it would be rented to the local doctor on a non-profit basis. The idea was born in May, ground was broken on August 28, and by December 1, Dr. Noyes had moved in. A better example of coordinated, cooperative, community-wide effort would be difficult to find.

As to strategy, a circular describing the proposed project was first mailed out to all patients who had been served in the past by Dr. Noyes. Thereupon, a personal visit was made to each and contributions received. Arrangements were made with six or more adjacent school districts to furnish volunteer workers on certain days throughout the construction period; local women served forenoon and afternoon coffee daily; noon meals were provided in Ceresco homes; and local businessmen spent their evenings digging trenches and cleaning up around the construction site.

The total cost of the project was $9,100, which included $600 for lots. The one-story pine and stone structure is 24×38 feet in size and houses a reception room, office, laboratory, X-ray room (equipment to be installed later), three consultation rooms, and a heating plant.

Medical Extension Programs. The second objection to rural practice, as voiced by Dean Murphy's students in Kansas, was the fear of losing contact with the fast-moving currents of medical progress. How can a general practitioner in an isolated region keep in touch with the latest developments in his field?

It is to the credit of young American medics that this question looms large in their thinking. And it points up a major responsibility that rests upon the shoulders of every contemporary school of medicine throughout the nation. The day is past when an institution of higher learning can bid its medical graduates farewell without further thought of educational service to them. In an earlier, slower-moving day the traditional program of training might have sufficed, but now the information acquired by a medical student in his formal college years grows rapidly out-of-date or incomplete.

The required education of a doctor is frequently said to take seven or eight years. This is a gross understatement. His education must be nothing less than lifelong, and there is cause for concern wherever the over-all curriculum and program of a College of Medicine do not reveal a clear awareness of this fact. Progress is being made. In a statement (January 28, 1954) to the Committee on Interstate and Foreign Commerce of the U. S. House of Representatives, Dr. Walter B. Martin as President-Elect of the American Medical Association referred to a growing emphasis upon postgraduate education and refresher courses to keep physicians abreast of the latest medical developments. During 1953, he indicated, nearly 1,600 postgraduate courses were offered by the nation's medical schools, medical societies, hospitals and other health agencies.[11]

The Division of Graduate and Postgraduate Medical Extension, University of Utah College of Medicine, and the Utah State Medical Association have developed a new approach in the field of postgraduate medical education which has special significance for doctors practicing in isolated rural areas. Audio-Visual Seminar Kits have been prepared containing medical discussions recorded on long-playing ($33\frac{1}{3}$ rpm) records, suitable illustrations and color photographs on 35 mm. slides, and

11. See "Our Positive Program," p. 7. Published by the American Medical Association, 535 North Dearborn Street, Chicago 10, Illinois.

a table-top slide viewer. All the physician needs is a record player to bring these medical lectures to his office or home. A transcript of the lecture, an index of illustrations, and directions for operation are supplied with each Kit, all for a fee of $5.00 plus freight charges.

All recorded lectures are given by authorities in their fields. The seven topics currently available for circulation, such as "Lesions of the Cervix and Vulva" and "Radiological Examination of the Chest," are of immediate interest to the general practitioner. Dr. Robert S. Warner, Director of the Division, reports that this phase of their postgraduate medical education program has been very successful.[12]

Improved Placement Services. The small community in search of a doctor benefits greatly from an efficient placement service. The American Medical Association has established a placement bureau to serve as a clearing house for information in answer to requests from physicians seeking a location and from communities seeking a physician. Placement programs are now in active operation in at least 37 states, and at least 32 are sponsored by state medical societies.[13]

A few years after its organization in 1946, the Virginia Council on Health and Medical Care established a placement service which has become highly effective. The Council "makes a point of not looking for communities that need doctors. It waits for communities to request guidance. Once a community has applied for assistance, the Council's director makes a personal study of the area and supplies a list of physicians who have indicated receptiveness to calls to settle in such communities. Where a community and a physician find each other mutually acceptable the Council exercises a follow-up service. The Council keeps juniors and seniors in Virginia's two medical schools informed on the placement service and follows any who take internships in other states with letters and information en-

12. Letter of September 10, 1954, to the author.
13. "Our Positive Program," p. 9.

couraging them to return to Virginia for practice. It also maintains liaison with interns who come to Virginia from other areas."[14]

The shortage of doctors in rural areas of the United States is at least to some extent a matter of unbalanced distribution. A placement service cannot be expected to solve this problem entirely, but it certainly provides an essential preliminary service in making the seeking community and the available physician aware of each other. A small community should use every available resource of this kind which operates in its region. If none exists, there is work to be done in getting a placement service established, and there is nothing quite so effective as constant pressure from the people themselves in getting a needed program under way.

Expansion of Training Facilities. The extent to which the deficiency of rural medical care inheres in a general shortage of physicians throughout the United States is not entirely clear. The American Medical Association points out that for "more than twenty years the supply of doctors has been increasing at a faster rate than the general population. . . . Today we have a total of 220,104 physicians—the largest in our history. Of this number 159,120 are in active practice. All the rest, except for about 9,700 who are retired or not in practice, are serving American health needs in research, teaching, hospitals and government service. On the basis of an estimated population of 160,000,000 in 1953, we now have one physician for every 727 persons, or approximately one physician actually engaged in the practice of medicine for every 1,000 persons. For the fifth consecutive year (1953-1954), the total number of students enrolled in approved medical schools has established a new record. The number of students graduated constitutes the largest group ever graduated in one academic year."[15]

A somewhat less optimistic note is sounded by Kolb and

14. New York *Times,* June 19, 1953.
15. *Op. cit.,* pp. 4, 5.

Brunner, basing their comments on a publication entitled "Estimates of Future Physician Requirements, Health Service Areas," by Joseph M. Mountain *et al.* (Washington, D.C.: Public Health Bulletin 305, 1949). These two rural sociologists summarize the situation as follows: "Comparisons made for the total number of physicians and specialists for the whole United States from 1909 to 1949 would indicate that we are losing rather than gaining ground. In 1909 there were 1.49 per 1,000 population, in 1949 only 1.37, and the low point of 1.25 was reached in 1929. Estimates of shortages by 1960 would be far in excess of possible supply if ratios which prevailed in 1940 were maintained. There were three more class A medical schools in the United States in 1950 than in 1930, 79 compared to 76, but the enrollment per 10,000 people dropped from 1.75 to 1.65 in the period."[16]

As to nurses, there seems to be general agreement that a shortage exists. Concern over the situation prompted the American Medical Association in 1947 to appoint a committee to study it and make a report. The findings, together with additional data obtained from official nursing associations, led the A.M.A. to the conclusion "that in certain areas there is a need for construction of new nursing schools and for the modernization of existing facilities." Adding that the need is basically one which must be solved locally in the respective states, the A.M.A. nevertheless went on to favor legislation embodying: "(1) one-time federal grants-in-aid to states, based on the Hill-Burton Act formula and administrative machinery, for construction, equipment and renovation of the physical plants of nursing schools, on a matching basis, with no part of the funds to be used in any manner for operational expenses or salaries; (2) grant of federal funds to the Committee on Careers in Nursing or some comparable private agency to help support a nurse recruitment program, and (3) a temporary grant-in-aid program, not to exceed five years and administered by the states,

16. *Op. cit.,* p. 420.

to provide scholarships for advanced nursing education to aid in the development of a larger corps of teachers."[17]

The problem of expanding and improving the facilities for training doctors and nurses in any given state probably seems tangential to most small communities. Their attention is understandably focused on the immediate task of getting or holding on to necessary medical personnel today. At the same time, however, they could well be giving some thought to what lies ahead for the next generation. They, perhaps more than all others, have a stake in legislative proposals to make possible the training of larger numbers of young people for medical service.

Hospital Construction. Another important aspect of the small community's quest for improved medical care is hospital construction. Such facilities bring not only beds but serve to attract doctors and nurses as well.

A great milestone for rural areas was established in the Hospital Survey and Construction (Hill-Burton) Act of 1946, which provided federal subsidies, with special consideration to states with low per-capita incomes. Through a system of grants-in-aid the U.S. Government was enabled to pay one-third of the construction costs of all approved hospital projects and a similar proportion of the expenses involved in making the required preliminary surveys.

Envisaged under the program was the eventual development of general hospital service areas by regions, each of which would include an interrelated system of medical units of four different types. Centrally located in each region would be a *base* or *regional* hospital. This would be a major installation, with specialized facilities for teaching, diagnosis, and research. Related thereto would be a number of *district hospitals,* each of which would have its own satellite system of *rural hospitals.* The fourth type of medical unit would be local *health centers* which might cluster around the respective *rural hospitals* and

17. *Op. cit.,* pp. 9-10.

which would devote their attention largely to public-health work and to routine diagnostic or emergency cases.

Of considerable interest to small communities which are looking forward to hospital construction projects is a study conducted by Paul A. Miller and associates of Michigan State College in 1949.[18] The cases of 218 successful Hill-Burton hospital construction projects were carefully examined, with particular attention to the patterns of action involved. They found that in 32 per cent of the cases, "one person was credited with actively initiating a concrete plan"; in 28 per cent there were "several persons working together"; while in 12 per cent "an organized group was looked back upon as the primary initiator of the new hospital idea." This seems to underscore the importance of the *individual* in our democratic social order.

Among the most serious potential difficulties encountered, particularly in the early stages of these projects, were "the maintenance of communication between the official sponsoring group and the community-at-large" and "justifying the hospital to the community." This bespeaks the importance of a good public-relations program and the active involvement in the project of as many influential community groups as possible.

In making appeals to the community, slogans were widely used, such as "Health is a community responsibility." Four-fifths of the projects reported "the intensive use of face-to-face contact in promoting the idea of the hospital," with great emphasis upon "street-corner discussion and persuasion. . . . No less important was the use of newspaper articles and speeches to organized groups. Some projects developed house bills, posters, and radio programs, and a few employed relevant motion pictures."

To learn from the experiences of others, project leaders in one-third of the cases travelled to other localities where hospitals

18. Paul A. Miller, *Community Health Action* (East Lansing: Michigan State College Press, 1953). Quotations used in the following paragraphs are from Chapter 2, "Beds, Bricks, and People," pp. 20-33.

had been constructed. As an additional safeguard, "nine out of ten projects recommended the careful use of community surveys and outside consultants as worthy devices. . . . The evidence suggests that the initiation and organizational features of the hospital quest were conspicuously free of professional assistance from without the community. However, most projects found endless consultation necessary on the details of site selection, blueprint development, the actual construction, and the requirements of hospital ownership and administration."

Professional fund-raisers were employed in about one-sixth of the 218 projects, and it was interesting that in such instances the distinguishing characteristics of the campaigns proved to be "an extensive mobilization of human resources within an organization functioning as a temporary bureaucracy."

Whatever the method of fund-raising might have been, the optimum time-span for the campaign was ordinarily considered to be from one to three months, and it was not uncommon for a single campaign to yield insufficient funds for the hospital construction job. Where one or more additional campaigns were needed, the same method of fund-raising was seldom employed twice in succession.

The leadership of the 218 projects showed a striking uniformity. "Throughout the small towns . . . this leadership was provided by the men who manage the stores and shops and banks along Main Street. Although farm people and their organizations were indispensable, the hospital turned out to be the major concern of the businessman."

A final and highly significant lesson from the Michigan State College study is "the inference that community leaders for the hospital projects frequently were so intent on building the hospital that they overlooked the hospital operations to follow. In many instances, local people had come to believe that the big task was to gain the physical structure of the hospital. The rest would take care of itself." As a consequence of this preoccupation with construction, the question of "what to do with it" arose abruptly upon the completion of numerous projects.

Voluntary Prepayment Plans. Another event of recent years which may eventually prove of real assistance in making rural practice more attractive to physicians has been the rapid development of voluntary prepayment plans for medical and hospital care.

One of the headaches of the country doctor through the years has been the difficulty of securing prompt payment of the money due him from economically insecure patients scattered over the countryside. Anything that can be done to stabilize and simplify this economic phase of the doctor's practice is clearly to his advantage. Further, he is likely to be favorably inclined toward any program which encourages and helps his patients to secure hospitalization at the time they need it. Many prepayment plans now available are of benefit to the physician in this manner and, at the same time, serve the interests of the consumer by enabling him to budget a large part of his medical expenses.

Organized medicine is clearly on record as favoring this type of program.

> The American Medical Association believes that voluntary health insurance provides one of the best methods by which the average American can finance a substantial portion of his medical and health costs.
>
> For years we have advocated and strongly promoted the sale of voluntary health insurance as one of the aids to cushion the economic shock of illness. The growth of voluntary health insurance, which embraces benefits for hospital, surgical and medical expense, has been phenomenal during the past few years. By January 1, 1953, nearly 92,000,000 Americans had some form of hospital expense benefit insurance. At the same time, over 73,000,000 were protected by some form of insurance against the cost of surgical care and nearly 36,000,000 persons had coverage providing some medical expense benefits in addition to surgery.[19]

19. "Our Positive Program," p. 11.

Prominent among prepayment programs are the Blue Cross and Blue Shield plans which apply, respectively, to hospital bills and to doctor bills incurred in hospitals. In the year 1949, Blue Cross provided coverage for 37,000,000 persons, while Blue Shield reported a total of 18,000,000, but a majority of these subscribers were in urban centers.[20] Although marked progress has been made during recent years in rural areas, it must be kept in mind that "only 4.2 per cent of the populations of states that were over 70 per cent rural in 1945 participated in Blue Cross plans. The comparable percentage for states that were over 70 per cent urban was 18.7."[21]

At the Eighth National Conference on Rural Health in 1953, Dr. F. S. Crockett observed that "great progress continues in the [insurance] coverage of rural people and we can entertain a reasonable hope of its eventual servicing of 60 per cent or more, of those who should have it. The greatest challenge is how to bring the benefits of prepayment to the remaining 40 per cent. There is no easy, simple answer."[22]

It is possible that part of the answer may lie in the further development of voluntary prepayment plans which are designed along cooperative lines. Jerry Voorhis, Executive Secretary of the Cooperative Health Federation of America, has described the cooperative approach in the following words:

> So the job can be done and in many places is being done. This is the job of enabling all sorts and conditions of people to have and pay for the high quality medical care which American doctors, dentists, nurses, and technicians are able to provide. That is, all this is possible if certain conditions are fulfilled. These conditions are: (1) A considerable number of families must be willing to pool their present and future need for medical care together and

20. Kolb and Brunner, *op. cit.,* p. 431.
21. Loomis and Beegle, *op. cit.,* p. 733. See also Mott and Roemer, *op. cit.,* p. 482.
22. "Looking Back to Look Ahead" (mimeographed address, Council on Rural Health, American Medical Association), p. 7.

pay for it ahead of time on a regular budgeted monthly basis. (2) Arrangements must be made with a balanced group of doctors—including both family doctors and specialists—to provide the care needed by these families. (3) The care must be preventive as well as curative; its aim must be to keep people well, not just to cure them after they are sick; and it must extend to the whole family. (4) There must be initiative, effort, and a sense of ownership and responsibility on the part of members and subscribers to such plans. (5) The doctors must control all the practice of medicine, and the economic aspects of the plan must be controlled by or on behalf of the patients.

Where these conditions are present, voluntary action by the people and their doctors can solve the health problem which America as a nation faces.[23]

Improved Public Health Programs. A final subject to which rural communities might well give thought in their efforts to secure and retain medical personnel is the public health program. A sound public health program supports the work of the physician and makes any community a more attractive and satisfying place in which to practice.

Ensminger and Longmore have briefly summarized the rural situation as follows:

Public health work has been organized on a county basis, and in most cases the county has proved to be an effective unit for health organization. The number of county health units with a full-time county or district health officer grew from 606 in 1932 to 1,874 in 1947. In addition to the health officer most of these county health units have a sanitary inspector, a visiting nurse, and a clerk. A staff of this size can render effective public health service in a county of under 25,000 population located in an area of less than five hundred square miles. The health unit personnel conduct health examinations of school children, give immunizations, and carry on various clinics of a specific nature. The nurse teaches hygiene, child care, and first aid in the home, and also serves in

23. *Information Letter,* Cooperative Health Federation of America (343 South Dearborn, Chicago 4, Illinois), July-August, 1954, p. 4.

emergencies. Other functions of the public health unit include: (1) school inspection; (2) coordination of all health services; (3) organization of maternal and infant hygiene measures; (4) treatment of venereal diseases; (5) inspection of milk supplies; (6) inspection of water supplies; and (7) general inspection of public food preparation.[24]

The Social Security Act of 1935 gave tremendous impetus to the public health movement in the United States. Our Federal Government now supports financially a wide variety of public health services throughout the nation, making possible the development of reasonably adequate programs in all states where the cause has strong local support.

Always advantageous is a good working relationship between the various levels of governmental public health units on the one hand, and the many voluntary agencies which are active in this field on the other. Among the latter are the American Public Health Association, numerous state public health associations, and untold health committees in local organizations such as community clubs and councils. The governmental and voluntary public health units make a good team which should be employed in joint endeavor to the fullest extent possible. This gives the physician a favorable environment in which to work.

24. Taylor *et al., op. cit.*, pp. 173-74.

13

CULTURAL OPPORTUNITIES

Well done is better than well said.—POOR RICHARD'S ALMANAC

ONE OF THE DEFICIENCIES frequently stressed as inherent in the small community is the lack of cultural opportunities. Any city of moderate size generally provides a continuous array of concerts, plays, art exhibits, literary discussion groups, lectures, and the like, but what does the small community have to offer? The latter can certainly not hope to equal the city in performance.

It is encouraging, however, to see what individual small communities have done along this line. In fact, there is ample reason to believe that tremendous possibilities for richer living exist in all rural areas where people have the necessary vision and a willingness to work cooperatively toward common goals. Cultural opportunities have to be *created,* and the power to create lies within human beings everywhere, whether they are rural or urban. True, the small community has definite limitations in its relatively small population and modest economic base, but even so there is much that can be done.

It is the purpose of this chapter to describe how certain small communities have approached the problem of cultural enrichment and to point out a few of the many resources which can be tapped. Perhaps the examples cited may serve to counteract the attitude of defeatism on this point which is all too prevalent in rural areas.

THE TYLER PUBLIC LIBRARY

From the earliest days of our country, rural residents have had difficulty in gaining access to reading materials from public library sources. Through various devices such as state travelling libraries, regional libraries, county libraries (with local stations serviced by bookmobiles), township libraries, community libraries, and joint township-city libraries, the situation has shown improvement over the years. Yet even as late as 1941 there were sixteen states in which from 70 to 89 per cent of the rural population was without free public library service.[1]

The problem is still far from being solved. Too common still are the small towns whose public library facilities resemble that of a Kansas county seat described by one of the author's students: "I was in high school and was looking for a book on geography for outside reading. Although I have always loved to read, I had never been in the library before. It was probably due to the fact that it is only in a little wee corner of an old building that has been condemned by the fire department as a fire hazard for as many years as I can remember, and also it was only open a few hours a week. As I went in, I could see no file or other indication of the manner in which the books were shelved. So I asked the librarian about the book and she replied: 'I don't know. It could be around.' I asked her where that type of book would be found and she indicated a certain corner. It was so dark I could hardly see with the dim light. In the small aisle where one barely had enough room to walk, much less turn around, I began looking where she had indicated. There I found children's story books. The books were in no order whatsoever that I could see. They resembled a shelf of children's books after they had just thrown them in, yet this would go on record as a library!"

One of the most serious problems of the small-town library is that of keeping it open a reasonable number of hours during

1. See Anderson and Gross, *Can Towns Have Better Library Service?* (Chicago: Rand McNally & Co.).

the week without excessive cost. Where sufficient volunteer help is available this problem may not be acute, but difficulties in procedures often arise where several such workers are used. How, if it must therefore use paid personnel, can the small community afford to keep its library open throughout the week?

A unique scheme has been functioning effectively for several years at Tyler, a village of 1,100 population in southwestern Minnesota. In a combination which at first glance may appear ridiculous to the observer, the Tyler Public Library is housed with the Community Cooperative Locker System. Every person who goes to his locker for meat must first pass through the room which contains on open shelves the 2,000 volumes of the Tyler Public Library. He passes through again on his way to the street. This means that the library is open to the 2,500 people of the community (town and farm) during the same hours as the meat locker, a total of 57 hours per week. It means, further, that a larger proportion of the total population passes through the library during any given week than perhaps through any other building in town. The patrons come in just as they are—the farmers often with muddy or snow-covered boots—to the lockers in the rear, pause long enough on the way out to select a book or two, and leave with nourishment for both body and soul tucked under an arm. As a matter of principle, there are no fancy rugs or furnishings to discourage browsing by patrons.

The entire library is operated on an honor basis. The borrower removes a desired book from the shelf, signs his name to the card in the book, stamps a "due date" two weeks distant on the card and on the slip in the back of the book (using a date stamp which is adjusted each morning by the supervisor of the locker system), and finally drops the card into a slot in a small box. To return the book, he simply drops it through the slot in a larger wooden box. At regular intervals, usually after business hours, a librarian comes in to replace all returned books to the shelves, to send "overdue" reminders to the borrowers concerned, and to straighten up the library in general. For this she is paid $35.00 per month.

The checking out and returning of books is thus an entirely personal matter for the borrower, who is free to steal if he so desires. The nine-member Library Board states that book losses have been relatively slight, rarely exceeding 25 per year. The cost of replacing these volumes is nominal, it adds, in comparison with what it would have to pay to have a librarian on duty during the 57 hours of weekly operation. Circulation is nearly 6,000 per year. The project is financed by an annual 2-mill levy on village property which provides, over and above the salary of the librarian, about $500 to cover the cost of new books, rental of quarters ($10.00 per month), and various minor items. Only books which are read are retained on the shelves.

It should be clearly understood that the Tyler community makes no pretense at operating a reference library, which certainly could not be handled on this basis. It is simply an arrangement for securing maximum circulation of good literature to the homes of book lovers at a cost which the village can bear. As such it is functioning very efficiently. An earlier attempt to obtain a county library arrangement had failed, and the present plan was worked out as next-best.

Big Springs Concert Series

The wide-open spaces and sparse population of the western Great Plains are hardly conducive to elaborate programs in the cultural arts. In a penetrating article entitled "Space As A Social Cost," Anton H. Anderson has stressed that cultural opportunities come at a relatively high price in areas where population density is low.[2] The price is high, not only in terms of financial outlay per individual served, but also in terms of the time and effort which must be offered by the people concerned to attain

2. See *Journal of Farm Economics,* Vol. 32, No. 3 (August, 1950), pp. 411-30.

their goals. In such regions ingenuity and devotion are essential to the development of programs.

In the panhandle of western Nebraska is a small town of 500 known as Big Springs. People of vision in that locality had been irked for some time by the necessity of travelling to distant cities in order to enjoy the personal appearances of outstanding stars of the concert stage. They recognized the handicaps of a small western community in drawing major artistic talent, but were determined to work out some arrangement under which the big names in music could be brought to town.

They were persistent, these "visionaries," or they would have been stopped in their tracks by the ominous voices of warning. "Nothing of this sort has ever been done in a community as small as yours!" "Where did you ever get the crazy notion that people in these parts will come out to hear your 'long hair' performers?" But they forged ahead and have now completed five successful seasons, each of which has seen five remarkable performances featuring talent such as Frances Greer and Brian Sullivan of the Metropolitan Opera Association, and a Viennese Ballet Ensemble—yes, in Big Springs! The programs have been of consistently high quality, purchased at a cost of $750 to $1,000 apiece. The concerts are held in the Big Springs community hall, a wooden structure seating 1,000 people.

It is not uncommon for communities to play up this type of program as a money-making tourist attraction, but this is not done in Big Springs. In fact, it is extremely difficult for outsiders to gain admission to the concerts because all seats are sold out on a season-ticket basis several months in advance of a concert season. The program is publicized only among the farmers, ranchers, and townspeople who live in that region, and there is little fanfare.

Here's the story, in brief. Ed C. Klemme runs a small electrical appliance shop in Big Springs. He likes his business, and he also likes good music. Together with others of similar cultural interests he began to examine the possibilities of overcoming what sociologists call cultural inadequacy in his home community. It was obvious to this nucleus of forward-looking people that the thing they had in mind could not be attained by Big Springs working alone. Instead of then dropping the idea, they went on to discuss the matter with friends in neighboring communities on the assumption that "if we can't do it by ourselves, perhaps we can swing it by getting together with others." These discussions resulted in the formation of the Platte Valleys Civic Music Association, a group of eight Nebraska and three Colorado communities dedicated to a common goal.

Each spring the Association holds a kick-off dinner in Big Springs, where plans are laid for a one-week membership campaign which follows immediately thereafter. Through the work of a volunteer team in each of the eleven communities, 1,000 memberships are sold for the coming fall season. Annual membership dues are $5.00 plus federal tax, and admission to concerts is limited strictly to members of the Association. Since overhead expenses are small, the Association each year has about $5,000 available in advance for the purchase of artistic talent. The concerts have consistently drawn full and enthusiastic houses.

It is noteworthy that the folks in these eleven western communities are not exceptional at all. They are ordinary rural Americans who are attempting to enrich their community life by employing a technique as old as man himself: cooperation.

Rural Art Programs

People in some rural areas of the United States are not as concerned today as they formerly were about "cultural inadequacy" in the world of art. Certain institutions of higher learning have developed fascinating rural programs for encouraging artistic endeavors and for bringing travelling art galleries to outlying communities. Among these are the University of Wisconsin and the University of Nebraska.

James A. Schwalbach has described the Wisconsin program as follows:

> Wisconsin plans to put as many paintings in the state as there are dairy cattle. Sponsored by the College of Agriculture, the Wisconsin Rural Art Program has exhibited 1,800 pictures this year. These were painted by the citizens who handle the Guernseys and the Holsteins, the Shropshires and the Lansdownes, the Poland China and Duroc hogs, the Plymouth Rocks and the Leghorns, and the growers of oats and barley and potatoes. . . .
>
> Most of the rural artists are in their middle years, with a few going toward the setting sun. But there is not one of them who is not aglow with the joy that comes from capturing some particular beauty of the world. Back of certain pictures lies a determination to put down some scene beloved by parent or grandparent. . . .
>
> The rural art program begins to function, so far as the University is concerned, about February 1, provided the snows are not too deep. The state has been divided into twelve sections so that no one who wants to paint is too far from a regional art center. Every Friday night when rural art is cooking, a car sets out from the Wisconsin campus. It holds a professor from the art education faculty, also this author, whose business it is to make rural art flourish, and two graduate students or seniors in the art department. The next morning the four university art experts meet the local rural artists in a church, a schoolhouse or a town hall. Already the pictures the local artists have made are on the walls.
>
> The professor of art immediately goes into action, giving a demonstration while the rural painters crowd around. He may make a water color of the landscape he sees out of the window, or he may create a block print before his audience. He may make a pastel portrait or even an oil.
>
> In the afternoon there is a talk on a general art subject and then, working together and using every means of holding an audience, the art professor and the graduate men give a comprehensive gallery tour.
>
> "You have to be on your toes," says Fred Logan of the art de-

partment. "These people are really interested . . . they want to find out what art is and how to arrive at it."[3]

The Art in Extension program in Nebraska is sponsored jointly by the Department of Art, the University Extension Division, and the Agricultural Extension Service of the University of Nebraska. Since its inception in 1936, thousands of people in rural communities have availed themselves of the opportunities afforded to enjoy treasures of art or to cultivate their own artistic talents through the program of travelling art galleries, lectures, off-campus classes, and workshops which covers the state.

One element of the program is a Nativity Gallery portraying great works of art centered about the birth of Jesus. During the two-year period 1952-54 there were 87 Home Extension Clubs which used this gallery, 1,740 rural women seeing it and taking part in a lesson dealing with it.

Among a number of other galleries available is a Senior Art Exhibit, the purpose of which is to "acquaint the lay-person with recent developments in art," and to "help children and adults to become more sensitive to works of art" by viewing and studying original productions from their state university. During the same two-year period, 6,775 people attended the showings of this exhibit in twelve different communities.

A unique feature of the program is a loan exhibit of framed pictures which are available for display on the walls of individual homes in farming areas.

A travelling International Art Exhibit of Children's Work is a recent development of inter-cultural significance. With the help of the foreign services of the U. S. Government, the University and the Nebraska Art Association assembled a fascinating collection of pictures drawn or painted by children in all parts of the world. A farm scene from India, for example,

3. James A. Schwalbach, "Wisconsin Rural Art Program," *Town and Country Church,* October, 1952, p. 8.

depicts a lad milking a cow from the left side, and the young artist carefully explains in an appended note that "although in the United States you may milk from the right side, no Indian cow would permit such goings on!" Colorful and widely divergent scenes are portrayed, each in its own cultural setting. The International Art Exhibit is currently being circulated among all communities which desire to have it—another example of the opportunities for cultural enrichment which are available to rural people who take the trouble to inquire.

Carnival Caravan

An unusual non-profit program, designed to promote the wider distribution of cultural opportunities in rural communities, was initiated some years ago in New York State under the name Carnival Caravan. The project has been described by Earl J. McGrath, former U. S. Commissioner of Education, as "an excellent procedure for stimulating local interest in life-enriching recreational and cultural pursuits."

The originator and organizer of the Carnival Caravan, Barbara Chapin, has characterized the program thus:

> Today we too often tend to sit back and let events wash over us—a natural defense with so much happening, the refusal to be involved. But it isn't exciting, nor is it fun to remain forever the objective observer. . . .
>
> To introduce cultural activities with top-flight exhibitions and demonstrations, plus the showing of materials and instruction as to how such activities can be developed in your own community, is the work and purpose of the Carnival Caravan. This really is a mobile community center, designed to take creative recreation to rural communities.
>
> The Caravan travels on special trucks which will set up in your town (for a five-day period) just as a circus does—giving local folks, among other things, an opportunity to: set type at a printing press; watch binding; examine fine book exhibits; browse; hear story hours, authors talk, reviews—the Bookbrigade; watch a play, act in short skits and charades; make up stories and drama-

tize them—the Playhouse Story Book; dance, sing, debate; give recitals; watch professionals do all these things; hear concerts—the Music Hall; see fine exhibits of art, crafts, industrial design; show their work; try their hand at weaving, pottery, drawing, painting; watch demonstrations, chalk talks—the Gallery; see foreign films, cartoons, documentary and training films; hear special records—the Cartoon House.

There are also places for recordings, puppet shows, strolling musicians; food stands for simple refreshments; and a play school where you can park your child with confidence.

Let's be perfectly honest about one thing—the amateur and the professional worker will not be confused. You may pitch a mean curve in sandlot baseball, and have the time of your life doing it, but you don't expect to be asked to replace Bob Feller in the big league.

The Carnival Caravan will bring exhibits of the best work being done to remind you just how exciting and skillful this or that art can be. When you pick up a lump of clay, you are not expected to turn in a masterpiece, but you should enjoy the feeling of having some form grow beneath your fingers. Local work will be shown informally, and in every town will be found one or two craftsmen working at high professional standards.

In other words, some of the cultural advantages available to city dwellers can now be enjoyed by the rural towns and villages that hang out the welcome sign for the Caravan. In fact, the idea grew from a concern for the lack of opportunity afforded the rural child in the field of cultural learning.[4]

The keynote of this type of program is community involvement, not only in terms of active citizen participation in the Carnival activities themselves, but in joint sponsorship of the project by local civic, professional, and social organizations. The essential goal is to encourage increased creative activities in towns and villages. As Miss Chapin puts it, "We want to take them a 'tickler'—and we are looking forward to the time when we leave behind us in towns all over the country young-

4. Barbara Chapin, "Carnival Caravan," *Recreation,* October, 1949.

sters [and oldsters] who say, as did one small boy studying an abstract painting at Chautauqua: 'Gee, I never knew there was anything like that in the world. I'm going to take a whack at that myself!' "[5]

Drama

Hundreds of small communities throughout the nation find inspiration, wholesome recreation and creative experience in dramatic productions of many kinds: plays, skits, pantomimes, operettas, pageants, and the like. Not infrequently these productions are actually written by residents of the communities drawing upon local subject matter, and this makes them doubly significant.

During Minnesota's recent centennial year, to take an illustration, there were many communities and counties which presented elaborate historical pageants, dramatizing their progress from pioneer days to the present time. This type of production provides not only an interesting show for spectators but ordinarily involves the active participation of scores of local residents in digging out historical data, in planning and writing the script, in finding appropriate costumes, in developing the music, and in a host of other essential preparations, as well as in the actual performance itself.

The town of Minden, Nebraska (population 2,120), known as "the Christmas City," has developed a superb system of Christmas lighting and each year presents a Christmas pageant which draws crowds of up to 10,000 people. The real importance of this annual event, however, lies not in the number of outsiders attracted, but in the creative experience which this production provides for the Minden people themselves. It helps to make this community a better place in which to live.

The Little Theatre movement has struck root in many rural communities. With stimulation and encouragement from the state university, about 750 plays were written in Wisconsin

5. *Ibid.*

during a recent four-year period, dozens of new community theatres were organized, and more than 75,000 individuals participated in dramatic productions during a single year (1950-51).[6]

While such drama programs ordinarily contribute to well-rounded living in small communities in a relatively inconspicuous way, it occasionally happens that sensational events occur. According to a newspaper account in 1954, the Village Players of Shelby, Nebraska (population 624), had "now that it is Spring . . . embarked on another season of dramatics. And all is quiet. Last year a dispute on stage props got out of hand, swelled beyond the Players and into the village itself. Artist Terence Duren had painted Greek figures on the props. Immediately some persons in the cast declared the paintings weren't properly clothed. Others in town took sides. Outcome was that the Players, despite threats that the play would not be staged, played before full houses. The local issue, however, had come to the attention of the world and the Players received newspaper clippings on the subject from Rome, Paris and London." . . . It's a small and interesting world.

6. See Kolb and Brunner, *op. cit.,* p. 391.

14

BEAUTIFICATION

A thing of beauty is a joy forever.—JOHN KEATS

ORDINARILY, THE PROBLEM of making the small town more attractive physically resolves itself into two principal tasks. First, there is the matter of eliminating eyesores, and second, the implementation of projects to improve appearances through landscaping and other devices. Let us examine each of these.

Generally speaking, the small town is a far less attractive place than it ought to be. To an entirely needless degree, one finds unpainted buildings, uncut weeds, miscellaneous rubbish on vacant lots, unkept lawns, conspicuously located automobile junkyards, and other unaesthetic features. The elimination of such blemishes is in certain respects a responsibility of local governmental officials whose duties include the maintenance of streets, the control of weeds on public property, and the regulation of land-use in the village.

The first of these, street maintenance, is usually handled reasonably well because of the close correlation between unattractiveness and inconvenience. Chuckholes on Main Street are not only an eyesore but a source of daily irritation to the shoppers who must drive an obstacle course to avert damage to tires and wheels. Public pressure mounts rapidly under such circumstances and remedial action is taken with minimum delay.

The cutting or spraying of weeds in public areas is also handled fairly well, particularly in the larger villages. There are many smaller places, however, in which the only concern is to prevent the spreading of seeds, and where this is true, the cause of "the village beautiful" suffers.

A perplexing land-use problem for local governmental authorities in many small towns is the control of junk yards, particularly as to location. From the aesthetic viewpoint the existence of a junk yard on Main Street, in a residential area, or anywhere, for that matter, where it is not concealed from view, is unfortunate. The fact that so many eyesores of this kind exist in conspicuous places bespeaks the seriousness of the problem.

The American Society of Planning Officials has the following to say on this subject:

> The regulation of junk yards is a problem in nearly all cities. On the one hand, the junk yard is a necessary enterprise—the basic unit in a multi-million-dollar salvage industry which, among other things, supplies an indispensable raw material for the steel industry. On the other hand, it has been traditionally felt that the junk yard has undesirable characteristics. The principal problems of the junk yard from the point of view of the municipality include noise, unsightliness, odors and smoke, dirt and dust, rats, and other insanitary conditions. The attempts to regulate junk yards fall into three general types: zoning ordinances; licensing ordinances which establish requirements for the legal operation of a junk yard; and ordinances declaring junk yards to be a nuisance and prohibiting or restricting them on that basis.
>
> Zoning ordinances normally restrict junk yards to locations in one or more industrial districts, usually with some sort of qualifying regulation. In 25 per cent of the zoning ordinances analyzed by ASPO, junk yards are permitted in light industrial districts—on the condition that the business be conducted wholly within a building, or on a lot, surrounded by a "solid fence or wall" (usually six to eight feet high) which would effectively screen the yard from view. Some zoning ordinances require that

before a junk yard can be located even within a district in which it is permitted, there must be a public hearing on the application. A very few zoning ordinances allow junk yards to be operated in business, commercial, or even in residential districts, with permission granted after a hearing. Junk yards with the status of nonconforming land uses under the zoning ordinances have been allowed up to five years to remove to a permitted location or to erect fences; in the majority of the ordinances examined, the time limit stated is from one to three years.

A municipality may license junk yard operations in the same way that it licenses other occupations and trades. While the *location* of junk yards can be controlled through the zoning ordinance, the special junk yard ordinance is the more useful device for establishing and enforcing standards of design and operation. In such licensing ordinances, requirements have been written which: forbid the burning of trash (unless in approved incinerators); require fences or walls of specified heights and materials; require the control of rats, flies, etc., on the premises; limit the granting of licenses to persons of known law-abiding character, and forbid the purchase of goods from minors, intoxicated persons, thieves, or "fences"; require that a complete and accurate record be kept "in the English language" of all transactions, which is examined by the police at regular intervals; provide for inspections to insure compliance with the regulations before granting or renewing licenses.

A number of smaller communities have passed ordinances defining junk yards as public nuisances; with that point established, the business is excluded from the municipality.

The precise form which these regulations take varies from state to state, and within a state, depending upon the type and extent of authority granted the municipalities by their respective legislatures.

As for the legality of these regulations, the courts have differed. In at least one case a court threw out a junk yard ordinance on the ground that it was unreasonable and excessive exercise of the police power to require that all junk yards, regardless of location, be bounded by a solid board fence. The court said that such a fence would not remedy any unsafe or insanitary conditions which

> could not be better corrected by other means. The courts have generally held that aesthetic considerations are not a sufficient basis for use of the police power, although this attitude is changing in some states—notably New Jersey, Florida, Texas and Louisiana. It has also been held that a junk yard is a "legitimate and useful business" and does not become a nuisance merely by so stating in an ordinance. As a general rule, ordinances regulating junk yards must be reasonable and have a definite, obvious and real relationship to the police power objectives—the furtherance of public welfare, order, health, morals or safety.[1]

Regardless of the approaches used by local governmental authorities, they seldom move very far beyond the standards set by home owners and social organizations in relation to the elimination of eyesores. Hence the importance of strong interest along this line by both governmental and non-governmental elements of the community.

In addition to encouraging and supporting local authorities, voluntary groups and individuals can do much to help eliminate blemishes in the community. The mere fact that a prominent organization, for instance, shows concern about a given situation often provides sufficient incentive for an offender to take remedial steps. In one case, a villager who for years had kept hogs in what otherwise might have been a scenic spot, voluntarily decided to reorganize his agricultural pursuits when the Women's Club made it clear to him that they were quite unhappy about the public display of his porkers.

Where group pressure proves ineffective, it is sometimes possible for an organization to obtain permission from the recalcitrant to correct the situation for him. A case in point might be a Garden Club project to plant a row of evergreens along the edge of a conspicuously located junk yard, thus concealing it from view and creating a beautiful stretch of trees besides.

1. *ASPO Newsletter,* September, 1953, p. 69. Published by the American Society of Planning Officials, 1313 East 60th Street, Chicago 37, Illinois.

Or, to cite a second example, the old unpainted building owned by Mr. Stubborn on Main Street can be given its much needed dressing-up by a detachment of spirited volunteers from the Commercial Club, wielding paint brushes the full length of Main Street on a designated "paint-up" day.

One of the most common and effective methods of marshalling local resources for the elimination of eyesores is the annual or semi-annual "clean-up, paint-up, fix-up" week. The strength of this approach lies in its all-inclusiveness. Every type of physical blemish in the community becomes a target, and every resident has a social obligation to act.

In most communities there are some people who keep their property in well nigh perfect condition, always neat and orderly, and there are others for whom that goal does not even seem to exist. The behavior patterns of these two extreme types are not altered particularly by a community-wide clean-up campaign, but for the general run of people it can be highly significant. The average citizen is a person of good intentions who plans to trim his trees, paint his fence, and clean out accumulated rubbish "some afternoon" but who experiences considerable difficulty in actually coming to grips with these tasks. For him, the community-wide campaign is a real help because it relieves him of all responsibility for making the awful decision of *when* to swing into action. Further, the job becomes more pleasant for him because everyone else is similarly engaged and a sort of community momentum carries him along. In addition, he is more likely to do his work thoroughly, because the eyes of his fellow citizens are upon him as his are on them.

The sponsorship of clean-up campaigns takes many forms. In some localities the mayor issues a proclamation, while in others the Garden Club, or any other civic organization, may spearhead the movement. Where a community council exists, serious consideration should be given to sponsorship or promotion through its channels. Since all organized elements of a community are represented on a body of this type, a project which requires the cooperation of everyone, as a clean-up campaign certainly does, would seem to be a natural endeavor for it to assume. This was found to be true in Ashland, Nebraska (population 1,700), where the Garden Club proposed at the first meeting of a newly organized community council that the latter body assume active responsibility for the "clean-up, paint-up, fix-up" week which they had sponsored in the past. The result was that a moderately successful program of years gone by now became eminently successful, winning national recognition for its thoroughness and quality during the very first year of community-wide sponsorship through the community council.

When a community has established a system whereby it is tidied up at regular intervals, however, its work of beautification is only partly done. The long-term task of making it a more attractive place through the planting of flowers, shrubs and trees, for example, remains. In this respect, the hamlet can do as effective work as any larger locality. A case in point is Ormsby, Minnesota (population 183), where a railroad and highway right-of-way at the edge of town was turned into a garden spot which has become a source of joy to local residents and travellers alike.

The Heavenly Blue Climbers Garden Club of Ormsby was organized in 1939 and affiliated soon thereafter with the State Horticultural Society. There were eight charter members, all country women except one, who was a retired farmer's wife. A nurseryman from Sherburn, a neighboring town, helped to organize the club and suggested as an initial project a roadside park at the east entrance to the hamlet. At that time this entrance was anything but a beauty spot. Soon thereafter, a new state highway was built at the east edge of town, running parallel to the railroad and providing an excellent spot for a small park between the railroad tracks and the highway.

By 1943, when the Club had grown to a membership of sixteen ladies, it was agreed that they would go ahead with the project. A decision was made to plant shrubbery and flowers there, but since the Minneapolis and St. Louis Railroad and the State of Minnesota each owned a portion of the property concerned, it was clear that permission for the project would have to be obtained. The M. & St. L. gave its approval promptly, and the State Department of Highways investigated the site, requesting that the Heavenly Blue Climbers meet with the Ormsby village council to get its approval and a guarantee of maintenance for a period of twenty-five years. When this was done, the state then agreed to develop a landscaping plan for the area. After approval of the plan by the Club members, the state plowed the land, supplied and planted the trees, evergreens, and lilac bushes, and seeded the park grounds. The grounds were then ready for flower beds, three of which were prepared and planted by the ladies. Later, two more were added, one of tulips and one of peonies.

As one Club member put it: "We now have five beds. Each spring we buy and plant pink and white petunias with a white sweet alyssum border. Last fall [1953] we planted over 200 tulip bulbs in the beds. This spring, together with the lilacs, it was a beautiful sight to all passing by and a fine reward to our members for their efforts. Time and again the village council has expressed its appreciation for this spot of beauty at the entrance to our town, and the Club has received newspaper recognition and many fine compliments from people both far and near. In 1952 the same procedure was taken to extend the park to the opposite side of the entrance to the village. This time the ground was worked by the husbands of some of our members, and again the Department of Highways supplied and planted the trees and shrubbery, using the same plan as the first. It is in the hearts and minds of our members that soon we will prepare and plant flower beds here also. Each year, incidentally, the Garden Club makes a financial contribution to the village to help pay for the upkeep of the grounds."

Perhaps with its eyes on the Japanese Cherry Blossoms of our nation's capital, Sutton, Nebraska (population 1,353), launched a project to transform itself from a rather ordinary-looking town into a "city of flowering trees." For two years the Sutton Garden Club had been talking about this idea, and when a community council recently came into existence, the "flowering tree" proposal struck root, and all organized groups in the community are now cooperating on the project. There is no way of knowing at this writing whether the Sutton dream will eventually materialize. It is mentioned here only to emphasize the *dream* as an essential starting point for any worthwhile community project. Every existing beautification program was originally conceived in the mind of man and then translated into action.

Of course, the small community is limited in what can be done along this line and should not permit its dreams to run wild. However, the main trouble in most places is that people have far too little imagination, rather than too much.

It should be pointed out also that community beautification activities are in no way restricted to Garden Clubs and similar groups. Often a single homeowner can set an example which attracts the favorable attention of neighbors and eventually elicits similar action toward aesthetic goals. Much can also be done through flower shows, newspaper articles, school projects, and other devices to stimulate progress toward more attractive small communities.

One thing is certain: most small towns would be far more satisfying places in which to live if careful and consistent attention were given to this problem.

15

THE SMALL COMMUNITY: A SOCIAL FRONTIER

The greatest of faults, I should say, is to be conscious of none.
—THOMAS CARLYLE

THE FRONTIER IS A FAMILIAR CONCEPT in a country as young as ours. Memories of the great westward movement are, in fact, still vivid in the minds of many who personally experienced the challenges, joys, and sorrows of life in the undeveloped hinterlands. During the course of the century which ended about 1890, the vast areas west of the Appalachian Mountains had been populated, and the free land nearly exhausted. Crowning a series of legislative acts which had made land progressively easier for the pioneers to obtain, Congress in 1862 passed the Homestead Act, whereby any family head who was a citizen or desired to acquire citizenship could obtain 160 acres of land simply by living on it for five years. Great numbers of venturesome, freedom-loving souls left the settled regions of the East to break the virgin soil and build a new society in parts unknown.

The story of how this broad land frontier was developed has been ably told by scores of people in poetry, prose, and song and will not be recounted here. Suffice it to say that the frontier represented a great challenge to an energetic and resourceful people, driven onward by what James Truslow Adams many years ago termed the *American dream,* the dream of a "better, richer, and happier life for all our citizens of every rank, which is the greatest contribution we have as yet made to the thought and welfare of the world."[1]

This American dream has by no means faded with the passing of the land frontier. It is much in evidence today in relation to a wide variety of equally significant *cultural* frontiers. Note, for instance, the tremendous drive toward new discovery and invention in the physical sciences. Unbelievable as it seems, mankind so far has probably only scratched the surface of nature's wonders, and our modern comforts of life are only an inkling of what lies in store.

Equally limitless are the frontiers in the social sciences where men of scientific training are working tirelessly to probe the depths of individual human behavior and of social relationships. As further data are brought to light, the possibilities of abundant living for all are enhanced.

In the spiritual realm, a man would be rash indeed to regard the frontier as closed. The human being is created with genuine capacities for spiritual depth and growth, but somehow he ordinarily fails to develop them fully. A glance around the world and a moment's silent meditation regarding one's inner self is convincing proof of this. But here again society is hard at work —through church, home, and school—to push back the frontier.

The quality of life in a small community is dependent in large measure upon the degree to which its people are alert to developments on these cultural frontiers and are actively involved in helping to meet the challenges posed. In a sense, the small community may itself be looked upon as a social frontier, whose further development holds promise of richer human living. The trouble in many places is that people do not recognize the possibilities of growth which exist. Some mistakenly look back upon a "golden age" which, in reality, lies in the future as a goal toward which progress is possible. Others

1. James Truslow Adams, *The Epic of America* (New York: Triangle Books, 1941), p. viii.

think of the small community as a sort of static social entity which has attained its full, if stunted, stature and somehow stands on the sidelines, by-passed in the stream of social progress.

The future of the rural community rests with those leaders and followers who are aware that a frontier exists, who recognize that something can be done to develop it, and who firmly believe in local action as a means of forging ahead. Where this triple outlook prevails, there is ample reason for optimism.

Unfortunately there is no formula which a community can follow in its efforts toward self-improvement. The following suggestions, however, may be of interest. They have been drawn from a rather intimate association with many small communities over a period of years.

Maintain community pride. This is a minimum essential. Regardless of how large or small your community may be, there is little chance of forward movement if a wholesome community pride does not exist.

To be sure, there are two varieties of pride which must be carefully distinguished from each other. The one—a most regrettable brand—is characterized by a tendency to whitewash everything in the community, with a consequent blindness to weaknesses of all kinds. Here is superficiality at its worst. It precludes an honest admission of existing needs, without which no community can progress.

It is another type of community pride, however, which concerns us here. Inherent in it is a love of community which runs so deep that existing faults, instead of being sugar-coated or disregarded, are faced openly and squarely, in order that they may be overcome. It involves a constructive dissatisfaction with things that are not as they should be. The progressive small community possesses a community pride which is fully integrated with a constant alertness to things that need to be done.

Do not feel apologetic for living in a small community.

Remember that many large urban centers are now attempting through city planning procedures to break their huge masses of population down into various types of "neighborhoods." What they are really attempting to do is to recapture some of the qualities of the small town which have long since been lost.

Have faith in yourselves. Self confidence is as important for the small community as it is for an individual. In either instance, its lack represents a major obstacle to effective living.

Our type of society is founded upon the belief that the common man is capable of acting intelligently in his social relationships and that he can be trusted to do so. It is further based on the belief that democracy begins at home, which means simply that democracy is made or broken in the day-to-day grass roots relationships of our local communities throughout the nation. If rural Americans really believe in these principles, it is inconsistent for them to doubt their ability to solve their community problems.

To have faith in oneself, of course, does not imply an unwillingness to utilize help from outside sources. Such help is needed in many ways by the forward-looking small community. The important thing to keep in mind is that the only genuine concern for the welfare of any given community rests with the people who live there, and it is their own ingenuity and resources which must be paramount in any community improvement program. The outside expert can be valuable, but only in the sense that he helps to release and give proper direction to local energies.

Keep community spirit strong. Community spirit is difficult to define but easy to detect. Its presence or absence explains in many instances why certain communities are "up and coming," while "nothing ever happens" in others. Basically, it probably involves a recognition of self-interest goals in the attainment of a better community. The person who sees in a more fully developed community an opportunity for richer personal living for himself and his family is more likely to display community spirit than he who feels that he has nothing to gain. In attempting to build community spirit it is therefore important to help all local citizens to identify themselves with the major goals of the community.

Progress in the small community is peculiarly dependent upon the presence of community spirit because, as indicated above, so much of the work to be done is of a voluntary nature which must be accomplished by joint effort if it is to be considered at all. In this very fact lies one of the great satisfactions of living in rural areas. The thrill of achievement derived from an all-out cooperative effort to construct a lighted ball diamond or a community medical building, for example, is seldom experienced by urban residents, who normally acquire such facilities by paying taxes and watching the contractors at work.

Community spirit is apt to remain strongest where everyone cheerfully assumes his share of the work to be done and enjoys working with others. To "let the other fellow do it" is to undermine the very spirit which moves a small community.

Make self-analysis and self-evaluation regular features of group activity. The ancient Greek philosopher Socrates was undoubtedly thinking of the individual person when he said "know thyself," but his advice is equally pertinent for the small community. Knowledge of self is an essential for any community, particularly where its efforts at community improvement are concerned. A major portion of such efforts in a rural community are implemented through voluntary groups of one kind or another, and it is therefore important that such groups operate as efficiently as possible.[2] For lack of self-scrutiny, they

2. Helpful discussions of this subject are found in the following publications: Mark S. Matthews, *Guide to Community Action* (New York: Harper & Brothers, 1954), Part I: "An Effective Community Organization." Irwin T. Sanders, *Making Good Communities Better* (Lexington: University of Kentucky Press, 1950), "Part Four: A Better Community through Better Organizations."

often limp along in a discouraging manner.

The following Canadian "Parable of the Community Club" should sound strangely familiar to many types of social groups in the United States:

> In a certain place (many leagues away of course) there was once a Community Club. This Community Club held a meeting every week. At every meeting there was always a program. Once a year the members of the club elected a Program Committee to serve them and their affairs. Some of the members would argue over the actions of the Program Committee and there was much dissatisfaction. Other members would say, "Why agitate yourselves? The Program Committee is chosen from the members. It is up to them to direct the program."
>
> Then it happened that the Program Committee, hearing of the dissent and unrest among the members, took counsel together to plan a program that would be the envy of all who heard about it. They said, "We will choose a Topic and call upon a famous Speaker, one who is known throughout all the land and has gained great fame." This they did. They also secured a Film to please the members. The Program Committee, having planned so diligently (and thinking in their hearts that their meeting would be a model for all clubs in those parts) worked hard to spread the news of the great event around by tongues and the written word.
>
> But on the evening of the meeting there was also a Curling Event, and there had been a Box Supper the night before, and there was a Big Dance the same week and so when the hour of the meeting had arrived there were present the members of the Planning Committee, the Speaker, and ten others. The Committee was wroth and cried, "Where are the others? Do they not know we have planned the meeting for their benefit?"
>
> Even so, the meeting was commenced and the Film was shown. The Speaker was introduced and he gave a Talk which took quite a while and provoked much thought. When the Talk was ended the chairman called upon the members present to ask questions of the Speaker. Several times did the chairman exhort the members to ask questions but they held their peace.

> When the meeting was ended the members made their way home in twos and threes talking and arguing among themselves. And the Program Committee walked home in great disappointment saying, "These people are Not Interested. They are full of Apathy." And becoming more agitated still, some scornful of the members and some merely desperate, they said "How do you Interest people? How do you overcome Apathy?"[3]

Why do organizations have problems like this? The fundamental answer in any given case is rarely a surface phenomenon. Almost invariably, however, much light can be thrown upon the situation by careful *analysis* and *evaluation*. The folks involved in the above parable were eventually successful in working out their problem, and it was done by studying themselves and their organization in a realistic and objective manner. The questions which proved most helpful in this process were these:[4]

"Are the needs and interests of the members discussed frequently and understood by all?"

"Does the program provide real satisfaction to the members?"

"Do all the members get an opportunity to actively help plan, participate in, and evaluate program activity?"

"Are all suggestions and ideas from the members given equal consideration and respect?"

"Do the members know each other well, and maintain a friendly informal relationship with each other?"

"Do the members discuss frankly and openly the things they don't like about the group and its program?"

"Is there variety and stimulation in the method of conducting activities?"

"Do the members have difficulty in using their [meeting] time effectively?"

3. Written by Jim Ward in the June, 1953, issue of *Saskatchewan Community*. Published by the Adult Education Division, Department of Education, and the Saskatchewan Arts Board, 1100 Broad Street, Regina.

4. *Ibid.*

Determine your community's appropriate roles and try to excel in them. One of the most puzzling problems confronting the small community in a changing world is that of determining what services it can logically offer to its people. This is true in virtually every institutional field. Unfortunately the services offered in the past are not a safe guide today. The fact that a high school, a bank, or a creamery has existed through the years is no indication that it can or should exist today, nor is it a foregone conclusion that non-existence or failure in the past precludes successful operation today.

In resolving this problem, the process of trial and error has long been an important tool and will continue to be, but it is costly in terms of both economic and human values. Objective analysis prior to decision-making can lessen its impact by offering guidance as to the feasibility of contemplated action.

In regard to this matter the small community must pay close attention to its relationships with neighboring communities. Each rural community is becoming more and more an integral part of a larger social system involving a number of other communities, and the services that can be offered by any one are determined at least in part by those which are available in others. The implications of this for small-town business, discussed in Chapter 7, are pertinent also for most other types of services characteristic of rural community life.

At Cordova, Nebraska (population 147), a 12-grade public school had existed for many years, but the much larger educational institutions in nearby Friend and Exeter had grown increasingly competitive as time went on. After much discussion, pro and con, the Cordova people decided to drop their high school program. They resolved simultaneously to tear down the old frame structure which had housed all twelve grades and to replace it with a new modern brick elementary school building. They felt that, despite the loss of their high school, they were in a strong position so far as the lower grades were concerned, particularly if the facilities offered on that level were of the highest possible quality.

Here is sound strategy for the small community, whatever the institutional activity concerned may be: do your best, using any outside research aids that may be available, to ascertain what services are feasible in your community and then make an all-out and continuing effort to keep these services as efficient and attractive as possible.

Keep challenging goals constantly before you. One of the unfailing marks of a good community is that it possesses clearly defined ideas as to what must be done to make it an even better place in which to live. Goals are essential to progress in every area of human endeavor. Without them, stagnation prevails.

Tradition has its values in the life of the small community, but its relationship to human welfare is sometimes difficult to discern. Where a certain procedure is followed primarily because "we've always done it that way," it is time for reappraisal. Though the past is valuable as a partial guide to the future, it should never be permitted to assume a dictatorial position. Intelligent community planning, while deeply rooted in the past, is closely geared to realistic and challenging goals which lie ahead. It is in the progressive attainment of such goals that the real joy of community living lies.

INDEX

INDEX